Japanese Schoolgirl

CONFIDENTIAL

How Teenage Girls Made a Nation Cool

Brian Ashcraft with **Shoko Ueda**

TUTTLE Publishing

Tokyo | Rutland, Vermont | Singapore

Published by Tuttle Publishing, an
imprint of Periplus Editions (HK) Ltd

www.tuttlepublishing.com

Copyright © 2010 and 2014
Brian Ashcraft

ISBN: 978-4-8053-1255-1

Distributed by

North America, Latin America & Europe
Tuttle Publishing
364 Innovation Drive
North Clarendon,
VT 05759-9436 U.S.A.
Tel: 1 (802) 773-8930
Fax: 1 (802) 773-6993
info@tuttlepublishing.com
www.tuttlepublishing.com

Japan
Tuttle Publishing
Yaekari Building, 3rd Floor
5-4-12 Osaki
Shinagawa-ku
Tokyo 141-0032
Tel: (81) 3 5437-0171
Fax: (81) 3 5437-0755
sales@tuttle.co.jp
www.tuttle.co.jp

Asia Pacific
Berkeley Books Pte. Ltd.
61 Tai Seng Avenue, #02-12
Singapore 534167
Tel: (65) 6280-1330
Fax: (65) 6280-6290
inquiries@periplus.com.sg
www.periplus.com

17 16 15 14
5 4 3 2 1

Printed in Singapore
1402CP

TUTTLE PUBLISHING® is a
registered trademark of Tuttle
Publishing, a division of Periplus
Editions (HK) Ltd

Contents

She is the queen of cool.
She's a cold-hearted killer.
She's a popstar, an angel,
a saviour. She makes men
weak at the knees, and
makes women nostalgic.
She gives children hope.
She's a heroine for
gamers, a muse for artists,
and an inspiration to her
peers. The power of her
purse makes businesses
drool, while marketers
scramble for her opinion.
She's a trendsetting trail-
blazer, and a glimpse of her
country's future. She's a
symbol of feminine mystique.
She is the Japanese schoolgirl.

Schoolgirls, of course, are hardly unique to Japan. But I would be hard pressed to find someone here who disagrees with the manga editor who told me that Japanese schoolgirls make "an impact" on society—an impact that, I believe, is more profound and influential than that of school kids anywhere else on the globe. The question is why.

It's something I've been asking myself since I first started covering Japanese schoolgirls for *Wired* magazine back in 2003. It was my first paid writing gig, and because of it I had to read their glossy magazines, consume their culture, and pick their brains in the hope of tracking the latest craze. Schoolgirls got my foot in the door of a writing career, and for that I will forever be in their debt.

Yet whenever I revealed that I was doing a book about them, people reacted with raised eyebrows and coy assumptions that were clearly a carryover of stereotype and fantasy. I wasn't completely surprised. Japanese schoolgirls aren't only cool, they're objects of fetish. The Japanese Google site pulls up over 20 million results for *joshi kosei* (high school girl), and the English version is not far behind. Of course, this being the internet, a large chunk of those results are for pornography— which is an extreme manifestation of the power she wields over people. But getting mired in the fetish quagmire is to miss the bigger picture: the appeal of the Japanese schoolgirl is rooted in various emotional and sentimental elements of the nation's psyche.

For Japanese women, the appeal of schoolgirls is that they are in the prime of their lives, unfettered by work, marriage, and children. They are young and relatively free. For men, the appeal is the memory of a first crush, of sitting in a classroom surrounded by girls in skirts and sailor outfits. But the attraction isn't drawn across gender lines. Japanese schoolgirls, clearly recognizable in their uniforms, exist in an adolescent netherworld. They are not adults, and they are not children. Kids can look up to them, and grownups can look back at them as the last hurrah before entering adulthood.

The reach of the Japanese schoolgirl's power now stretches far beyond the domestic border. It's not enough that they are used today to advertise everything in Japan from bicycles and yogurt to (of course) mobile phones. The diffusion of Japanese pop culture across the globe— the notion of soft power epitomized in the brand of "Cool Japan"—found its most powerful icon in the images of uniformed schoolgirls in such fare as *Sailor Moon, Blood: The Last Vampire,* and *Neon Genesis Evangelion.* Western arbiters of cool have caught on too, as Japanese schoolgirls have been prominently featured in such high-profile films as *Kill Bill* and *Babel.* In fact, in a bid to ride the wave of her popularity, the Japanese government named a schoolgirl as a cultural ambassador to the world in 2008.

As I watched her power expand overseas, the question of why continued to nag me. The bid to answer it led me from the city streets of Tokyo's Shibuya shopping district to the rural countryside of Okayama prefecture. I interviewed some of Japan's biggest celebrities, most knowledgeable experts, and famous creators. I also talked to countless schoolgirls, on their way home, out shopping with friends, having fun. My collaborator and wife—herself, of course, once a schoolgirl—proved an invaluable source of insight into her own experience and the minutia of being a young woman in Japan.

And in the process of making this book, the obvious struck me. In asking about the impact of Japanese schoolgirls, I was actually asking about the power of all Japanese women—who either are, will be, or have been schoolgirls. And in thinking about modern Japan, it is only natural to think about this majority of the population and its makeup. The Japanese schoolgirl is both gruff samurai, strong and powerful, and demure geisha, beautiful and coquettish. Decked out in her Western-influenced uniform, she brings these elements together into a state of great flexibility—the ability to be strong or passive, Japanese or Western, adult or child, masculine or feminine. At home and abroad, she is a metaphor for Japan itself.

This is not fiction. The schoolgirl of the popular imagination and the cultural zeitgeist are informed and influenced by the real. Within real Japanese schoolgirls is a curiosity that drives their search for new stuff, the clear conundrum of yearning for both independence and acceptance, and always, of course, the subconscious awareness of just how ephemeral their time in uniform is.

Even with all the uncertainty of what will become of current schoolgirls after high school and what future fads and trends ensuing epochs will bring, one thing is dead certain.

They wield a mean bunch of cool.

Brian Ashcraft
Osaka, Japan

Note: The Japanese names in this book appear in the Western order, given name followed by surname. Japanese words have been written in the manner they most often appear in romanized text.

Sailor girls

If clothes make the man, uniforms make the schoolgirl. Whether it's those sailor suits with big red ribbons, blue blazers with striped neckties, or short plaid skirts and loose socks, the Japanese schoolgirl uniform is more than a wearable ID. It's a statement. With roughly 95 percent of high schools in Japan requiring them, wearing uniforms (*seifuku*) is not simply the norm, but a rite of passage, representing that carefree period in a woman's life when she makes the transition from child to adult.　　　>>

Tombow Uniform Museum

It wasn't always this way. At the Tombow Uniform Museum in Okayama, costumed mannequins are displayed in a timeline revealing the evolution of uniforms. The museum is Japan's only academic garb repository and sits catty-corner to Tombow's school uniform factory, where threads are fabricated for students across the country. Okayama is the uniform capital of Japan, and if you're wearing a Japanese school uniform right now, there's a seven out of ten chance it's from there.

The groundwork for mandated clothing in Japan was laid in the seventh and eighth centuries, when Korean- and Chinese-influenced imperial decrees compelled the classes to wear certain types of clothes. During the Heian Period (794–1185 AD), idle aristocrats were obsessed with seemingly trivial wardrobe matters like wearing the correct colored sleeves. When your days aren't spent toiling in a rice paddy, even the most minor fashion detail is important!

By the Edo Period (1600–1868), regular kids could study calligraphy, poetry, and Buddhism at their local temples. In a glass case at the Tombow museum, two smiling life-sized dolls are dressed in their regal study kimonos: one sits on the floor, and the other stands, grinning

Hello sailor!

Tsume-eri uniform

COURTESY UEDA FAMILY

FOLLOWING THE OPENING OF JAPAN in 1853 by the "Black Ships" of the US Navy, large numbers of foreign experts in a myriad of fields and industries were brought in to dispense their knowledge. Western fashion also began to be adopted, and leading the charge was the Meiji Emperor who posed for photographs in French-inspired military garb, complete with a sash, fringed epaulettes, and a breast full of medals.

France and the US served as influences for the new educational code of 1872, which established a national school system and made education compulsory. By the end of the decade, male students at the newly established Gakushuin University were sporting navy-colored school uniforms called *tsume-eri* (high collar), or *gakuran* (which loosely translates into "Western uniform"). The high collar design covered the neck, making students hold their heads higher and giving the young men a stronger appearance.

The following decade at Tokyo University, tsume-eri with spiffy golden buttons instead of simple black hooks were introduced. While not a military uniform, the tsume-eri certainly had a whiff of the armed forces the Meiji government was ramping up—most notably the Navy, the service adored by the nation's kids. According to Katsuhiko Sano, director of the Tombow Uniform Museum, the reason the Navy seemed so romantic was because sailors went overseas and had an international world view (while civilians could face the penalty of death for traveling overseas). "Boys' school uniforms started from that desire to emulate naval heroes."

Say I love you with a button

AT GRADUATION, high school girls ask their favorite male squeeze for the second-from-the-top tsume-eri button. Why the second? Out of all the buttons on the jacket, it's closest to the heart, that's why. *Swoon!*

Prince Albert Edward in a sailor suit, by Winterhalter, 1846.

ear-to-ear. These "study clothes" were threads donned for learning, but not strictly enforced or even uniform per se. For something to truly be a "uniform" it needs to be exactly the same, and that wouldn't happen to Japanese school clothes until the late nineteenth century.

ॐ ॐ ॐ

At the Tombow museum hangs a copy of an iconic 1846 portrait of the then Prince of Wales, Albert Edward. The future King of England looks about four years old and is decked out in a miniaturized sailor suit that looks uncannily like what Japanese schoolgirls wear today. The painting caused a sensation in Britain at the time. In an age when blue-bloods set fashion trends, soon children across the UK were suited up in sailor outfits. By the tail end of that century they were also the de facto threads for American and European kids. The nautical theme even spread to adult attire with seaside summer holidays very much in vogue.

During the Meiji Period (1868–1912), as Japan suddenly found itself playing catch up with the West, it began importing loads of foreign concepts, fashions, and technology, including the latest in military firepower. The military was short hand for modernization since Japan needed a modern military to become a modern power. Along with that came new uniforms, including European style naval outfits. Pretty soon boys in Japan were required to wear school uniforms inspired by the navy look. Girls, however, still wore kimono. But the snug, form-fitting kimono, while fetching, were designed for sitting on tatami mats—not in a chair hunkered over a desk, taking notes, and listening to a teacher. A change was needed. Some educators suggested the *hakama*, which were pants designed for horseback riding and worn by, gasp, men. Others, more forward thinking, proposed Western-style uniforms. That pitch was nipped right in the bud when the country's first Minister of Education—a British-educated advocate of Western clothing and culture—was assassinated in 1889. Worried that schoolgirls would be targeted for wearing Occidental outfits, a compromise was reached: young ladies would don balloon-like Japanese trousers. They looked like feminine skirts, but offered pant-like functionality.

That would change at the turn of the century when educator Akuri Inokuchi was sent abroad to research physical education at Smith College in Massachusetts. There she saw female students doing exercises in sailor-inspired "bloomers." When she returned to Japan in 1903, Inokuchi encouraged schoolgirls to get off their duffs and do gymnastics, and to do them while wearing the sailor-style outfits she had seen in the US. This was less to do with fashion and more to do with practicality as the bloomers allowed women to move freely. Two years later, after students at the country's national high school for girls began daily exercises in similar clothes, the look began to cling. Sailor outfits became synonymous with active wear, but it was not until the next generation of schoolgirls that the now iconic sailor uniform was born.

Sailor-style bloomers

Standing beside a display in the Tombow museum, Katsuhiko Sano points to a black and white photo from 1920, showing a schoolgirl in a long naval gown. "This is the first sailor-style school uniform for girls," he says. Sano should know. He not only tracked down that uniform, but also created the Tombow Uniform Museum to show how far uniforms have come. Thanks to Sano's detective work, Tombow was able to pinpoint this uniform from Heian Girls' School in Kyoto as the country's first. Unlike other school outfits or study clothes, these sailor-style, one-piece dresses were all identical and worn in class. But the one-piece design never really caught on.

In 1915, the headmistress of the Fukuoka Jo Gakuin—a Christian High School for Girls—was Elizabeth Lee, an American. "Ms. Lee was very beautiful," says Sano, "and all the students loved her fashionable sailor-style clothes and wanted to dress like her." The kimonos the girls had weren't exactly practical for study or physical education. A local tailor, Ota's Western Clothing Shop, began reproducing Lee's outfits for the spring 1922 class, complete with a ravishing beret. The Ota design made the rounds at other missionary schools, and in the pre-war era, the two-piece sailor suit became synonymous with Christian education. Best of all, the naval look of girl's uniforms dovetailed thematically with the naval inspired boy's uniforms. The two-piece design with a separate blouse and skirt

Heian Girls' School uniform

HEIAN JOGAKUIN UNIVERSITY

Elizabeth Lee

FUKUOKA JOGAKUIN JR & SR HIGH SCHOOL

became the blueprint for sailor uniforms and the design still used by learning institutions across Japan.

Meanwhile, in Okayama, the Tombow factory was producing split-toed socks called *tabi*, but having a hard time staying afloat. "Fewer and fewer people were wearing traditional Japanese clothes on a daily basis," explains Sano. The company needed another product and ended up ditching the socks to switch to

Fukuoka Jo Gakuin's two-piece sailor suit

school clothes. It was 1930—a time when it was common for families to have as many as five or six children—and the government was pushing education. Voila! Instant customers.

In the years leading up to World War II Japanese nationalism raged. Yet schoolgirls still wore Western sailor suits. (Though, when materials became scarce during the war, schoolgirls wore uniforms fashioned out of their mothers' old kimonos). Pants, however, replaced the skirts, with the rationale that it was easier to run from falling American bombs. Detachable padded hoods to protect against flying shrapnel were also necessary.

Schoolgirls during World War II

The war did little to stop the advance of the sailor suit as Japan got back on its feet in the post-war years, and it became part of the academic landscape. Other changes in the social fabric also had little effect on their spread. In the 1960s Japan experienced anti-war protests and leftist demonstrations much like those in the US and Europe. School uniforms were viewed as a symbol of Imperial

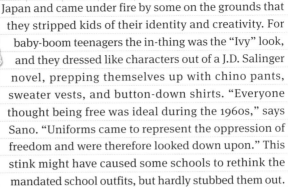

Sukeban style

Japan and came under fire by some on the grounds that they stripped kids of their identity and creativity. For baby-boom teenagers the in-thing was the "Ivy" look, and they dressed like characters out of a J.D. Salinger novel, prepping themselves up with chino pants, sweater vests, and button-down shirts. "Everyone thought being free was ideal during the 1960s," says Sano. "Uniforms came to represent the oppression of freedom and were therefore looked down upon." This stink might have caused some schools to rethink the mandated school outfits, but hardly stubbed them out.

In the confining parameters of school uniforms, however, kids were figuring out their own ways to show their individuality—with scissors! In the late 1960s and early 70s, bad schoolgirls in long skirts and Converse sneakers began cutting sailor tops short, exposing bare midriffs. The look was called *sukeban* explains Sano—slang for "girl gang leader." Not all sukeban chicks got in fist fights and knocked heads with baseball bats, but the delinquent look became iconic. The mere act of standing up to conformity by altering assigned clothing gave the most innocuous suburban rebel the air of danger.

Sukeban style marked the nascent stages of "uniform fashion" and soon schoolgirls everywhere were personalizing their apparel. While the first sukeban did the uniform altering themselves (or had their mothers do it), tailors soon began charging to shorten school tops. And when sukeban graduated, they'd embroider things like roses and Japanese kanji characters on the back of their sailor suits. Nothing says thorny rose like a schoolgirl who's going to punch your face in—or at least act like she will.

Sukeban boy

YAKKUN SAKURAZUKA not only knows what it's like to wear a schoolboy uniform, but just how comfortable a form-fitting schoolgirl uniform can be. Since getting into showbiz over ten years ago, the cross-dressing Yakkun has donned a sailor suit as part of his act. And not just any sailor suit but a hard-hitting *sukeban* version.

"I chose a sukeban style uniform," he says, "because I didn't want to be a weak, effeminate character, and the tough sukeban style was the farthest thing from that." Fitting for a tough guy-girl comedian who wields a wooden kendo stick and heckles his audience with biting barbs. But he's got a soft side too: "I love it when I'm confused for a girl, or when a woman says I'm pretty."

Yakkun Sakurazuka

In true sukeban style, Yakkun wears a long skirt and bare midriff with exposed belly button. "It's certainly made me more self-conscious about developing love handles." The first time he put on the sukeban sailor uniform, he was impressed how easy it was to move in the outfit. Still, the look took getting used to. "I kept stepping on my skirt when I was going up and down the stairs," he says.

Yakkun's collection consists of six outfits: two light summer uniforms, two heavy winter uniforms, one checked patterned uniform, and one white embroidered uniform. Some are order-made, some were presents from fans. "The best thing is that I don't need a wardrobe stylist," he says. "The worst thing is that the uniforms show dirt easily."

But the biggest difference between wearing girls' and boys' school duds is, according to Yakkun, the protection: "The male uniform isn't drafty during the winter."

Yakkun Sakurazuka, whose real name was Yasuo Saito, was tragically killed after being hit by a car on October 5, 2013. May he rest in peace.

TOP COAT CO., LTD.

By the 1980s, baby boomers who'd grown up when uniforms were frowned upon had children of their own, and when it came time to get the kids some learning, preppy school clothes proved very popular. School dress was conservative, and the sailor-suit standard found a new rival: the blazer.

Sport coats had been part of some school uniforms for decades, but it was in the mid-1980s that the blazer really took off. More than the "look," the practicality of the blazer and skirt drove its appeal. Students typically only bought a couple of sets of uniforms for all of junior high or high school. So for the first couple of years these may have been too big, but when girls hit a growth spurt the outfit would look terrific. In the final years of school, however, the uniform would be bursting at the seams. A blazer layered with a white shirt and a sweater vest was much more forgiving to raging teen hormones.

Blazer style

The preppy single-breasted jacket became very much in vogue—Tokyo schools leading the charge with navy and caramel colored versions. Large school crests sewn onto the blazers not only appealed to parents' preppy sensibilities, but breathed an air of nostalgia as the style was reminiscent of the jackets-with-embroidered-crests worn by the athletes of the 1964 Tokyo Olympics. In the "bubble" economy of 1980s Japan, the uniform moved well beyond simply functioning as a uniform—it became brand-name fashion.

Schools noticed a sudden spike in applicants when they changed their uniform designs. As a result, institutions across the country began adopting new styles. People like illustrator Nobuyuki Mori began to take a keen interest in the sudden variety of uniforms springing up at the time. While still in high school, Mori began sketching school uniforms

TOMBOW UNIFORM MUSEUM

The Illustrated Schoolgirl Uniform Guidebook, 1994 edition

in his neighborhood to quiz his buddies. When he left the 'burbs to study for university entrance exams in Tokyo, the endless uniform variations blew his mind. He noticed that no two uniforms were the same. They couldn't be, or else they'd cause confusion. So Mori set out to catalogue all this in the ultimate compendium, his 1985 book, *The Illustrated Schoolgirl Uniform Guidebook*, which would go on to sell two hundred thousand copies. "I was inspired," says Mori, "by all the different and beautiful uniforms in Tokyo."

But anyone who tried to keep up to date with uniform trends had a huge job on their hands. By the mid-1990s, preppy was out, and slutty was in. Schoolgirl skirts got short and white socks got loose. Much like the sukeban a generation earlier, girls rebelled against strict school uniforms. They wore outrageous makeup, dyed their hair, got fake tans, and rolled up their skirt's waistband to turn long dresses into D.I.Y. micro-minis. These dangerously short skirt–wearing, golden brown tanned schoolgirls were called *kogal* or just *gyaru*.

When girls began showing skin at more conservative institutions, parents and teachers gasped, and strict schools started scrutinizing scanty hemlines with before-class spot checks. Some private academies even went so far to have teachers scattered off-campus to eyeball girls on the way to school. Japanese students all carry rule books that outline their school's regulations, but the uniform fashion the girls were creating, says Mori, "exists in the space between those school rules and breaking them." Not all establishments gave a hoot though, and in some cases, delinquent girls were given carte blanche to run amok. In other cases the crackdown on micro-minis only encouraged the trend, and some girls started leading a double life. During learning hours, they'd unroll their skirts to an acceptable length; after school, they'd hike their cookie-cutter uniforms up and pull on a pair of loose socks, the other essential ingredient of the kogal look. It was clear girls enjoyed wearing their uniforms out of school hours, but only on their own terms.

Off to one side of the Tombow Museum is a large meeting room where staff from academic institutions and retailers sit in red fabric chairs and plan new duds with Tombow. Headless dummies model Tombow-produced uniforms for the Japanese clothing brands Olive des Olive and Comme Ça Du Mode. The meeting room is a lab of sorts as well, to research the latest school trends. The company not only polls teachers and parents, but also investigates schoolgirl tastes by quizzing kids. "Students want something they can wear after school," says Sano. This often means fashion that looks like a school uniform but that is, in fact, fake.

NOBUYUKI MORI

Illustration by Nobuyuki Mori

Uniforms by CONOMi

CONOMi

Diplomatically cute

IN 2008, the Japanese Foreign Ministry selected three women to be Ambassadors of Cute (*Kawaii Taishi*), including *seifuku*-wearing actress Shizuka Fujioka, who was nineteen. The Ministry hoped to capitalize on the popularity of cute Japanese things abroad and Fujioka saw her selection as a huge honor. "I think they picked me because I look good in a uniform."

Fujioka had already graduated from high school, where she was disappointed by her school's homely uniform. She now owns five sets of store-bought seifuku for her role, preferring the blazer and plaid skirt look, because, she says, "Sailor suits are way hard to coordinate!" She borrows the rest of her wardrobe from online retailer CONOMi, where she moonlights as an uniform adviser. "If you think school uniforms are cute," she says, "you shouldn't hesitate to wear them—even if you've already graduated from school!"

Her ambassadorial post ended in 2009, after a year of smiling and speaking at cultural events such as the Japan Expo 08 in Paris. According to Fujioka her role was to show the whole world "how cute Japanese school uniforms are." Mission accomplished.

Shizuka Fujioka

MOON THE CHILD

For girls in their mid-teens the uniform symbolizes a brief period in their life when they are free, unbound by adult matters like career, marriage, and children. There's schoolwork, sure, but as teenagers they are cushioned from the world around them. They're not children, and they're not quite adults—yet they have more freedom than both. Anything is possible. So many girls yearn to wear uniforms even when their schools don't require them. And if some girls think their own school's outfit is dorky, they change into clothes that, to the untrained

Uniforms by CONOMi

CONOMi

eye, look exactly like school uniforms. Whether it's during school hours or after class and weekends, the uniform is a blossoming beacon, bluntly signaling to society: I am a schoolgirl, young and free.

This demand has led some boutiques to hock cute, unofficial uniforms under the guise of "fashion" in order to side-step any run-ins with schools. Online retailer CONOMi, for example, special-izes in coordinating schoolgirl looks yet says it doesn't sell school-approved uni-forms, but rather, "preppy-inspired fashion." These faux uniforms are called *nanchatte seifuku* (just kidding uniforms). In 2008, CONOMi opened a store in the schoolgirl shopping paradise of Harajuku and launched an in-house clothing brand, arCONOMi, the following year. Some custom-ers even show up in full school regalia to get advice on the fine art of matching bows, vests, and plaid skirts or what necktie goes with their school-issued blazer. "My school's uniform was not so cute," says a twenty-one-year-old CONOMi staffer in full uniform get up, "and I always ached to wear fashionable school clothes."

⚜ ⚜ ⚜

Back in the Tombow museum, Sano is sitting at the table in the large meeting room, surrounded on all sides by mannequins in school clothes. When asked if he thinks uniforms will vanish, his reply is frank. "Not in Japan. Uniforms will always make the schoolgirl aware of what she is and her academic purpose. Japanese people take great pride in their roles in society. So, policemen should look like policemen. Nurses should look like nurses. And schoolgirls should look like schoolgirls." ⚜

勉強もスカートも、
やる気次第でまだまだのびるんだ。

もうすこしがんばりましょう

実は短すぎない方がカワイイ
17才 男子高校生

新潟県高等学校PTA連合会　新潟県高等学校長協会
制作：新潟デザイン専門学校

Japan's coolest skirts

ACCORDING TO URBAN LEGEND, the shortest school skirts in Japan are found in bitterly cold Niigata Prefecture, located off the Sea of Japan. While skirts started to inch down in Tokyo at the turn of the millennium, Niigata girls kept hiking them up until they hovered around eight inches (20 cm) above the knee, compared to Tokyo's six-inch (15 cm) average. These girls think nothing of walking through the snow with their bare thighs covered in goose bumps. The Niigata girls even accentuate their limbs by wearing short socks that show more leg.

While schoolgirls think the micro-minis are cute, the Niigata PTA doesn't, and they kicked off a "Proper Dress" campaign in 2009. Posters dotted Niigata school halls, telling schoolgirls that shortening their outfits was prohibited, and the PTA also distributed long-skirt propaganda that implied getting good grades and wearing tasteful uniforms were somehow connected.

Manufacturers like Tombow have even devised ways to keep schoolgirls from rolling up their skirts: such as waist bands so thick they're impossible to fold or when rolled reveal the school's unflattering crest. In Hokkaido, Sapporo's Municipal Minamigaoka Junior High School went as far as replacing skirts with slacks, which quickly stopped any short skirt problems. Stopped, we should say, until some girl rebel decides to take scissors to them.

Ironically the best defense against short skirts may prove to be cyclical fashion trends. In early 2009, the Japanese media noticed that girls in idyllic Nara, the country's ancient capital, were wearing 1980s-style long skirts and were even calling short skirts "dorky."

"Proper Dress" campaign posters

キレイめスタイル

そろそろ直せば？スカート丈

新潟県高等学校PTA連合会　新潟県高等学校長協会
制作：新潟デザイン専門学校

Get loose

THE MOST NOTORIOUS ITEM in the Japanese schoolgirl wardrobe would have to be loose socks. In the mid-1990s the kogal look was defined by them and they have come to symbolize a certain type of schoolgirl—one that is sexy, rebellious, and very cool. But originally, these infamous socks were American.

Eric Smith, an attorney by trade, hails from three generations of sock makers. In 1982 he started his own company, E.G. Smith, after adapting a woollen hunting sock design from his father's company. Eric changed the material to cotton, and managed to capitalize on the 1980s *Flashdance* fitness craze. By the early 1990s, the New York–based Smith was looking to expand and struck a Japanese distribution deal with a textile company in Osaka called WIX.

Various stories exist to explain how the socks then became popular with Japanese schoolgirls, including one that has schoolgirls in frosty Miyagi Prefecture choosing them purely to keep warm. But Smith and WIX company president Takahiro Uehori have another story. "Originally, we launched an E.G. Smith display at a SOGO department store in Yokohama in 1993," says Uehori. "Two high school girls bought the white boot socks and wore them to class. Before you knew it, the look had caught on at their school." Rigid school dress codes called for white socks, and Smith's socks were the antithesis of regulation tighty-whities. The boot socks—later dubbed "loose

ERIC SMITH

Eric Smith with fans of his socks

socks" for the way they hung—flattered short schoolgirl legs, making them appear long and slender. A fashion reporter noticed the Yokohama fad, penned a tiny blurb on the twelve-inch (30 cm) socks, and the trend spread across the country like a bad case of mono. "Loose socks weren't your typical short-lived teen trend," says Smith, "this one lasted ten years." Each generation wants something to call its own, and for girls during the 1990s, loose socks were it. "The self-expression became a uniform in itself," says Smith. "It expressed an entire generation of women."

Schoolgirls may have loved them, but schools didn't. "When loose socks first caught on," Smith says, "schools banned girls from wearing them.

Girls on the Street
on uniforms

I really like our school's sailor-style outfit. I've never been into *nanchatte* uniforms. But a different neck ribbon might be nice!

The best accessory? **Loose socks!!**

Stylish in loose socks at Tokyo Girls Collection!

Shiori Kaneko and Chinatsu Hasegawa

ANDREW LEE

Which only fueled their proliferation." Suddenly the socks weren't just a fashion statement, they were a national obsession. "On trips to Tokyo, I'd visit Shibuya Station at three in the afternoon," Smith says. "Schoolgirls would be changing out of school-regulation knee-high socks into loose socks to go meet their friends. I think this caused the loose socks to be fetishized by some businessmen."

By the mid-1990s, after reports that schoolgirls were meeting older men for *enjo kosai* (paid dating), loose socks were no longer just associated with schoolgirls, but with sex. Enjo kosai preoccupied the tabloids and the Japanese government. And by the end of the 1990s, new regulations cracked down on underage-sex-for-money. But schoolgirl characters were already turning up in porn films wearing loose socks, and massage parlors and sex clubs had young looking women decked out in the socks. The original rebellious meaning of loose socks had been twisted by the media so that even today they carry sexual connotations.

Stuck on you

THE SECRET behind how girls managed to keep their loose socks up? Glue.

In the early 1970s the president of chemical company Hakugen noticed his granddaughter fretting about her school socks falling down. In 1972, the company launched a roll-on glue dubbed "Sock Touch" that could be used to stick knee-socks to the skin of your calves to keep them in place. In the following decade fashion trends changed, however—skirts got longer and socks got shorter. Sock Touch lost its touch, and in 1985, Hakugen stopped producing the adhesive.

But when loose socks went supernova in 1993, the company took notice and re-introduced their Peanuts branded "Snoopy Sock Touch." After having its production halted for almost a decade, Sock Touch was a smash. Hakugen geared up its sock-glue production, rolling out Disney-themed Sock Touch, perfume-free-sensitive-skin Mild Sock Touch and Super Sock Touch, recommended for "furious sport-like movement."

HAKUGEN

Keep your socks up with Sock Touch glue!

Navy socks

Short skirts, navy socks

BY THE YEAR 2000, even the strongest Sock Touch could not hold up the popularity of loose socks. They were no longer a cutting edge high school trend, but rather something junior high kids wore in hope of seeming grown-up. Navy-colored knee-high socks were the next big thing. But even then girls needed a way to express themselves and chose socks bearing the logos of famous brands, such as Burberry, Polo, Vivienne Westwood, and even Playboy.

By 2013, however, some schoolgirls began wearing navy socks under baggy loose socks in a convergence of both trends.

CONOMI

Honey, I shrunk the uniform

WHAT BETTER WAY to remember your schoolgirl days than with your uniform... miniaturized? Tokyo wedding-dress company Petite Leda does just that. Mini blazers, tiny skirts, small sailor suits—you name it.

Petite Leda began crafting one-of-a-kind pint-sized school uniforms after blushing brides wanted a way to memorialize their student years. Former schoolgirls can have the company make the mini clothes from the original fabric—even using their uniform's actual buttons. For those unwilling to part ways with their precious schoolgirl threads, Petite Leda will find matching fabric. They'll even sew the former schoolgal's name on the miniature uniform's inside, just like the real deal.

According to Petite Leda, the 15-inch (38 cm) high get-ups are extremely tricky to make, with the uniform collars and the sleeves being the most difficult. Since each is different, there isn't a set pattern per se, meaning that Petite Leda's expert seamstresses must try to capture the essence of the original uniform as a small-scale replica. Quality craftsmanship like this ain't cheap: the pint-sized replicas cost 31,500 yen (US$320). The mini clothes are available as stand-alones or versions fitted to small teddy bears.

PETITE LEDA

Middle-Aged Sailor-Suit Dude

DURING THE WEEK, fifty-year-old Hideaki Kobayashi is a computer engineer, working on algorithms to solve image processing problems. On weekends, he's a Japanese schoolgirl.

How does a mild-mannered computer engineer turn into a schoolgirl? First, Kobayashi got interested in taking cosplay (costume play) photographs of manga, anime, and video-game fans dressing up as their favorite characters. When exhibiting his photography at a design event in 2010, and hearing that a well-known cross-dresser would be checking out his pics, Kobayashi decided to dress up as a schoolgirl. He was surprised at the positive reactions his outfit garnered at the event. But it wasn't until the following summer that he wore the outfit out among the general population when a ramen restaurant in Kanagawa offered a free bowl of noodles to anyone over thirty years old who came dressed in a sailor-type uniform.

"Nobody took up the ramen shop's offer in the first month," Kobayashi recalls. "A friend of mine recommended I go. I was the first one to get a free bowl of ramen." After that, Kobayashi was hooked and began wearing the outfit in Tokyo. Online, people began buzzing about a bearded man in a sailor suit. The gray-haired man in the cute schoolgirl uniform and the braided beard cut a striking figure. Middle-Aged Sailor-Suit Dude was born!

"The sailor suit is a symbol of cuteness," says Kobayashi. "I think it makes middle-aged guys feel nostalgic for when they were in school and had a secret crush on a female classmate. Well, that's what I imagine, because actually, I went to an all-boys school." Kobayashi wasn't a fan of the boys' school uniform, saying it made him feel "tied up."

Now that Kobayashi is an internet celebrity with his own website (growhair-jk.com), he's been able to parlay that into television appearances. He's even involved with a sugary sweet pop group called "Chaos de Japon,"

Sailor suit—symbol of cuteness

PHOTOS TAKEN BY HITOSHI WAKIRI

populated with actual junior high schoolgirls, not just as the group's photographer and one of its producers—he's also a fully fledged member. "Now, I have to follow the rule imposed on members: I'm prohibited from falling in love with someone," Kobayashi says. "If I were found violating the rule, I would have to shave my beard off."

Kobayashi isn't being serious. Then again, maybe he is. There's a certain playfulness about his sailor-suit schtick. It's unusual, sure. But it's also fun and oddly cute to see a middle-aged man in a schoolgirl uniform riding the Tokyo subway or flipping through a magazine in a bookstore. In a way, it breaks up the monotony of urban life. Here is someone doing what they want, instead of being constrained. For Kobayashi, the schoolgirl uniform is liberating.

"People are surprised when they see me in person, because they've seen me on the internet or on TV," Kobayashi says. "They rush up to me and ask to shake my hand or take a picture. That makes me feel good, and I feel like I'm doing something good in society too."

Chapter 2
MUSIC

Idol worship

On the eighth floor of the Don Quixote building in Tokyo's geek capital of Akihabara, throngs of AKB48 fans stand waiting outside a theater dedicated entirely to the famous all-girl pop group. Above them is a marquee proclaiming "Japan's most sophisticated show." The fans are mostly male. But a few girls dressed in uniform-like fashion—way too skimpy to be seen in school hallways—linger at the edges. Inside is a single row of seats reserved for female fans like these, and another row for families. On one wall of the lobby dozens of small brass plaques bare the names of the diehards who have attended over a hundred concerts, and there is little room for more. These fans worship AKB48 the way idols are meant to be worshipped, with an almost religious fervor. >>

AKB48's penthouse theater represents the pinnacle of success. But out in the streets of Akihabara there are plenty of wannabes. Sidewalk idols appear in the area singing gooey pop songs in hope of creating a grassroots fan base among the *otaku* (geeks or fanboys) who congregate there. These street idols are considered more "real" than inaccessible pop idols because regular folks can see them up close and personal. They are called *aidoru* (会いドル), a word play on the Japanese pronunciation of "idol" (*aidoru*; アイドル) with the Japanese kanji "*ai*" meaning "to meet." Interaction with fans is essential to their success: they hold intimate concerts, pose for photographs, sign autographs and even partake in handshaking events where thousands of fans line up to meet members, but only if they first purchase the group's latest single. AKB48 is a product of an era in which social networking sites seemingly make everyone accessible and everything personal. So far, it's working: in 2009, AKB48 set a record for first-week sales by female artists with the chart-topping single "River." In 2013 the group beat their own record, becoming the biggest selling female group in Japan ever.

Just like the girls struggling at ground level, the girls of AKB48 are approachable but just out of reach, and true fans would not have it any other way. "What if I did actually date an AKB48 girl?" says one waiting fan. "Then all my friends would be jealous and maybe even hate me. And what if dating her was not as I imagined? What if I was disappointed?" What if, what if?

AKB48 is the brainchild of Yasushi Akimoto, the lyricist and record producer of the original girl idol super group of the eighties, Onyanko

YOU, BE COOL!/KING

AKB48
River

Club. With AKB48 he has tapped into the desires of the otaku who hang out in Akihabara, with the "AKB" being short for "Akihabara" and the "48" referring to the number of group members (though the real number hovers close to ninety). The concept behind AKB48 is to offer fans a huge selection of girls to adore, make sure each girl has a different personality for fans to identify with, and make the girls perform live often enough for fans to see them regularly.

The group is split up into several teams, each of which take turns performing at the theater seven days a week. When they perform, they're typically in school-uniform-inspired outfits, while their music videos are often set in schools. AKB48 is *the* schoolgirl super group.

🌸 🌸 🌸

Sixteen girls in matching school blazers scuttle on stage. Pre-recorded music strikes up as they go into a choreographed dance sequence and start singing. They're young and cute. They chatter between themselves and banter with the audience, which reacts with its own performance—of chants and synchronized dance moves. The atmosphere is festive, everyone is happy, and the theater is throbbing. It's summer 2009, and AKB48 is on the verge of going supernova.

After the show, team member Rino Sashihara—decked out in a frilly light blue tutu, Mickey Mouse jumper, and white cowboy boots—ices down her calf. "There's a mosquito in here," she warns, "it stung me." Then adds in English, "Oh my god!" gesticulating wildly.

Rino Sashihara

Moeno Nito

COURTESY OFFICE 48

Tomomi
Nakatsuka

Rino has been an official member of AKB48 since October 2008. Ditto for her schoolgirl compadres Moeno Nito and Tomomi Nakatsuka, who are also taking a break between shows. "I was a fan of AKB48 a long time before I auditioned," the sixteen-year-old Rino says. "I love idol music. Onyanko Club were super!" She and Tomomi gush about following AKB48 before joining, while Moeno is frank: "I'd heard of them, but I wasn't a big fan or anything." She was, instead, into Gothic rock and decorating her nails.

"There aren't just lots of girls in AKB48, there are lots of different *types* of girls," Rino says. Tomomi, decked out in a track suit and sneakers, chimes in. "Yeah, there are cute girls, beautiful girls. Everybody is different. I think that's really what makes the group unique." Tomomi, for example, likes manga and video games, and Rino's hobby is eating *udon* noodles. Scan the profiles of other AKB48 members and you'll find girls into professional wrestling, horror movies, or anime. It's an idol smorgasbord where fans can find at least one idol to his or her taste. The music might be what draws folks in as listeners, but it's the girls who turn them into fans.

"The big difference between AKB48 and other mainstream idol groups is the interaction with the fans," Tomomi points out. "We try to make a connection with the crowd," Moeno adds. With weekly performances, TV shows, radio programs, recording and video shoots, the AKB48 girls are busy. "Sometimes it's hard to always be smiling and happy," Rino says with a wide grin. "Not that I'm horribly depressed— the furthest thing from it!" Sharing these feelings and personal issues with fans is something idols tend to avoid. It's too much information, and a total buzz kill for the escapism that idols buffs want.

❧ ❧ ❧

AKB48 perform at their Akiba theater

In the wake of World War II escapism and hope was provided by a trio of schoolgirls dubbed "*Sannin Musume*" ("three girls"). Hibari Misora, Chiemi Eri, and Izumi Yukimura made their name covering jazz standards and belting out entirely new Japanese creations. The three starred in a couple of MGM-style musicals together, and the biggest star, Misora—the Shirley Temple of Japan's post-war war era—captured the ears of a nation with her 1949 smash hit "Kappa Boogie Woogie." The East-meets-West ditty was about a mythical Japanese creature getting his boogie woogie on.

During the 1950s, American G.I.s and Japanese greasers alike rocked out to local cover bands doing their best Elvis impressions at live venues across the country. Covers soon gave way to original tunes and the first Japanese language rock songs. When rockabilly started attracting thugs and bikers, music producers decided they needed a new sound and a new look. Out went the leather, pompadours, and uncontrolled hip wiggling. In came clean-cut kiddies and choreographed dance routines. The "idol age" was dawning.

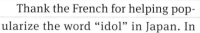

Thank the French for helping popularize the word "idol" in Japan. In 1964, the comedy film *Cherchez l'idole* hit Japanese theaters, and Sylvie Vartan's "*La plus belle pour aller danser,*" the movie's theme song, sold a million copies. As a wave of Gallic tunes from young, pretty French chanteuses were snapped up, cover versions of the Franco hits were released to capitalize on the trend. What the burgeoning Japanese idols lacked in French sang-froid, they made up for in cute.

It was in the 1970s that girl idols would truly come into their own. This new generation of Japanese popstars had grown up in a very different period from their parents. It was an era free of Japanese imperialism and American firebombing: the Olympics had taken place in Tokyo in 1964 and the World's Fair was held in Osaka in 1970. The future was *now*, and girlish dreams of becoming a pop star were possible. Unlike the matinee idols of the 1950s and 1960s, idols during the 1970s were created on television in living rooms across the country. On talent-search TV shows like *A Star Is Born!*, stars really were born. Schoolgirls like Momoe Yamaguchi, Junko Sakurada and Masako Mori were the top three idols of the day and the media dubbed them "The Schoolgirl Trio."

Junko Sakurada

Masako Mori

MINORUPHONE RECORDS

VICTOR RECORDS

Yamaguchi was only thirteen when she showed up to her first recording session in a sailor-style school uniform. She raised eyebrows in 1973 with songs like "Unripe Fruit," peppered with raunchy lyrics such as "You can do whatever you want with me," and "It's alright to spread rumors that I'm a bad girl." The suggestive songs she sang were in sharp contrast to her age, and the more conservative acts of other idols. The thrill for male fans was in the power of suggestion and her coquettish schoolgirl image.

JAS-2016
¥700

伊藤つかさ

少女人形

Tsukasa Ito's Shojo Ningyo

For these idols, image was everything, and everything was controlled as the idol grew into her role. The clothes. The hair. The likes and dislikes. Idols were the girls girls longed to be, and the girls boys longed to be with. According to media specialist Tatsu Inamasu, idols appear to be very pure, but they are actually doing something very impure: trying to get money from people's pockets. "The fans understand that the act is a lie," says Inamasu in his book *Idol Engineering*, "but they enjoy it. The whole thing is a fantasyland game." It doesn't matter if the idol can't sing. To be worthy of idolatry, the singer's talent doesn't have to be perfect—*she* has to be. It's easier to develop a strong attachment watching a pure, awkward young woman become an accomplished performer than simply seeing the final product. Fans want someone to root for, to cheer on. There's an emotional investment and gradually an I-knew-her-when nostalgia emerges.

The so-called Schoolgirl Trio had hit on a nerve. Throughout the 1970s idols appeared in print magazines and on record covers in their sailor suits—like on Nana Okada's 1975 top ten single "*Jogakusei*" (Schoolgirl). In the following decade the schoolgirl trend continued with the likes of TV star Tsukasa Ito, and her 1981 debut album *Shojo Ningyo* (Girl Doll). The title couldn't have been more apt. Ito was thirteen years old and, of course, appeared on the cover wearing a sailor-style uniform. Her name was scrawled on the album cover in childlike writing and when she appeared on music programs to promote the album everyone knew what she would be wearing.

A perfect schoolgirl storm was brewing. And it hit hard in 1985 when Fuji TV's late night program *All Night Fuji*—which had been using college-aged girls as eye-candy—hosted a special on high school girls. The program's producers created a schoolgirl band dubbed Onyanko Club (Kitty Cat Club) with a logo of a pussy cat bent over, flashing her bloomers. The bonus pun? "*Nyan*," is Japanese for "meow," and "to do *nyan nyan*" was 1970s slang for sex. None of this was lost on the show's predominantly male viewers.

The group's sound was heavily influenced by early 1960s American girl acts like the Ronettes, but instead of the Wall of Sound, Onyanko Club had the wall of schoolgirls. At their debut, there were eleven of them. Their first song, "Don't Make Me Take Off My Sailor Suit," was a top five smash, with blunt lyrics that didn't beat around the bush—the song contains doozies like "I want to have sex before all my friends." If the subject matter did happen to be lost on listeners, the "nyan nyan" refrain in the background would have clued them in. All this was coming from a gaggle of regular looking schoolgirls who didn't exactly ooze sexuality—which is exactly what the fans found so damn charming.

Even though most of their matter-of-fact lyrics were written by a man, (Yasushi Akimoto, who went on to found AKB48), and seemed to be aimed at legions of leering male fans, there was something oddly empowering about Onyanko Club. They didn't dress trashy, and they definitely did not let anyone

PONY CANYON

take off their sailor suits. They sang about telling their teacher to stop putting the make on them, or about calling out some pervert on the train.

They were good girls, ones you could admire, emulate, and dream about. But to make sure they stayed pure in the eyes of the public, Onyanko Club girls had to abide by a rather conservative set of rules: no boys; no dance clubs; no skipping school; no smoking. Normal high school stuff, you'd think, but these weren't normal high school girls. They were idols, and if they broke the rules the consequences were harsh.

Onyanko #4
Eri Nitta

COURTESY OFFICE WALKER

The no-smoking rule cost a handful of the group's original members their jobs. Two weeks after the first episode of the group's hugely popular after-school variety show *Yuyake Nyan Nyan* (Sunset Nyan Nyan), six of the original eleven members were embroiled in a smoking scandal. A weekly tabloid caught the underage girls puffing away at a coffee shop near their recording studio and all but one of the girls got the axe. The "Tobacco Incident" became a taboo topic of discussion—it would be bleeped out if it was brought up on air.

Suddenly, one of the remaining members, Eri Nitta, was thrust into the spotlight as the group's leader. While numerous celebrities start out as idols, many are reluctant to talk about their time as an idol, as if they are ashamed of how they made their careers. Not Nitta, who chats openly about her Onyanko Club days. She was seventeen at the time and had originally only auditioned because the five thousand yen a day paycheck (about twenty-five US dollars during the 1980s) was better than some dopey part-time gig after school. "I didn't set out to be an idol," she says, "but, before I knew it, I had become one." Even as the group was poised for superstardom, she had been mulling over leaving. But with the smoking scandal, the number of members dwindled to half; if Nitta quit there would only be a few left. "I wanted to be professional," she says about her decision to stay and see how things turned out.

Things turned out well. Really, really well. Onyanko Club churned out hit singles and had a hit TV show. Each Onyanko was given an ID number, and the group had a song in which each girl would introduce themselves by number. Nitta was number four but always went first—something she says she didn't like: "But I suppose being at the top of the heap is better than being at the bottom." The newly minted star found herself juggling normal schoolgirl life with being an idol. "Things got difficult when Onyanko became famous," she says, "but my classmates didn't suddenly change on me. They protected me, they supported me." The number of Onyankos swelled, and fifty-two girls became members over the course of the group's two-year lifespan—though not all at the same time.

Onyanko Club singles

Seiko Matsuda

POP MUSIC IN JAPAN can be divided into two epochs: Before Seiko Matsuda and After Seiko Matsuda. She was a new breed of idol, an über idol of sorts, and was dubbed "*burikko*," which means a woman who acts young and girlish to appeal to men.

Making her debut in 1980, she caused a sensation, belting out a record-setting string of twenty-four number one singles in a row. Her bobbed hairstyle was the most influential hairdo of the day with schoolgirls clamoring to get the iconic "Seiko-chan cut."

Super idol Seiko Matsuda

CBS/SONY MUSIC

Onyanko Club were a step towards the "real" idols that populate Akihabara today. People could identify with them, and cheer them on. They weren't the most polished singers, and they weren't the best dancers—heck, they weren't even good dancers—in fact it sometimes looked like the group had just learned their dance moves backstage. Besides the obvious appeal of school-aged girls singing about sex, Onyanko Club was popular because it was comprised of fairly normal young women. They were slightly awkward and seemed genuine, or at least, slightly more real than the previous generation of polished, overly controlled idols. The greener the better. "Before us, idols were dolls," Nitta says. "Today's idols are human beings. We were somewhere in-between."

In order to keep the group sown with fresh faces the group's TV show ran "idols wanted" notices, and new members would audition in what could be described as a beauty pageant of sorts, complete with swimsuit and talent competitions. To make room, Onyanko Club regularly "graduated" members in surprisingly depressing episodes of *Yuyake Nyan Nyan*—all before a studio audience of grown men.

Graduating members were marched out on stage, given flowers, and told to sing their way through Onyanko Club's standard showstoppers, a difficult task through the shower of tears and sniffles. Then, to a background of "Auld Lang Syne," they'd say goodbye to their cohorts. For the Fuji TV producers and managers, the hope was that these girls would then go onto be successful solo artists. A few did stay in show business. Others simply assimilated back into society, working as office ladies, becoming mothers, or even teaching yoga.

Two-and-a-half years after debuting, Onyanko Club called it a day, and the remaining members hung up their sailor suits. The final concert was held in September 1987 at Yoyogi National Gymnasium with present and former members alike. Everyone graduated, and Eri Nitta was the last member to leave the stage. It was a dramatic, fitting end to Onyanko Club after setting a trend for groups hoping to capitalize on the schoolgirl craze. Not surprisingly, the blueprint Onyanko Club drew up would be mastered by the biggest girl group act of the following decade, Morning Musume.

Morning Musume

✿ ✿ ✿

In 1997, the pop impresario simply known as Tsunku♂ —who writes his name with the Mars symbol—held live TV auditions to find a new singer for his band Sharam Q. He found her, but he also found five other girls who intrigued him but didn't make the cut. Their consolation prize was to be a founding member of the biggest idol group of the late twentieth century, Morning Musume (Morning Daughter). Before that was to happen, though, there was one condition: the girls had to sell fifty thousand copies of their first single in just five days. It was grassroots-marketing-meets-reality TV, with camera crews following the girls around as they tried to promote their then unknown group.

The public couldn't help but root for them, and with live concerts held in the cities of Osaka, Fukuoka, Sapporo, and Nagoya, Morning Musume finally broke the fifty thousand mark.

By 2003 the group had expanded to sixteen members, becoming so successful that Tsunko♂ quit his band to focus on managing these girls. But while the dapper Tsunku♂ was the public face of the band, the real

Morning Musume

mastermind lurked in the shadows. As the media-shy talent agency president Naoki Yamazaki said in a rare October 2001 interview with print magazine *Cyzo*, "I entrust all the music stuff to Tsunku♂. But which members graduate and who enters the group is all decided by me. The real producer isn't Tsunku♂, but me."

Over the years, Morning Musume became less of a band and more of a music institution, or better yet, a factory for churning out female idols. The group took its cues from Onyanko Club: lots of young

girls and graduating members. But they pushed it even further with Morning Musume spin-off groups and sub-units like Berryz Kobo (Workshop), and C-ute—which could be cross promoted on its morning TV program, *Hello! Morning*. All the singers belonged to the corporate label "Hello! Project," and even after they graduated they still remained signed to the group's talent agency to be filed away for another group or launched as a solo artist or actress. It was the Onyanko Club model perfected and expanded.

The same "no boys, no smoking rules" that governed Onyanko Club were very much part of Morning Musume's M.O. This helped keep the girls ideal and pure, but also magnified stupid teen mistakes into press circus fodder, something former member Ai Kago knows firsthand. "For idols," Kago says, "the most important thing is to protect your image." Tarnishing that image can change everything. In February 2006, a

Good Morning Musume!

NOT CONTENT with merely conquering Japan, Morning Musume has set its sights abroad. Taking the Chinese moniker "*Jou An Sao Nu Jou*" (Good Morning Girls Group), the troupe entered the mainland market in 2007 and added two Chinese-born singers to help seal the group's global appeal: twenty-one-year-old Junjun from Hunan and eighteen-year-old Linlin from Hangzhou, both now graduated.

Japanese tabloid magazine ran grainy black and white photos of the then eighteen-year-old Kago clutching a cigarette. Not only had she violated a group rule, but she had broken the law—smoking under twenty is illegal in Japan.

This wasn't 1985, so, unlike the Onyanko Club girls, she didn't immediately get the axe. But Kago's agency put her on a one-year suspension, "house arrest" as Kago calls it. She stayed in her hometown of Nara, near Osaka, until the agency invited her back to Tokyo, where she worked at their office taking phone calls, serving green tea, and learning about the idol business. Just as she was poised for her comeback, Kago was photographed holding hands with a thirty-seven-year-old married man. The tabloids jumped on the story of Kago and her beau at a hotel in a hot springs resort town. She admitted her indiscretion and was dropped by her agency. "The sad thing is that when I entered the entertainment industry," she recalls, "everything became too much of a fantasy land." Though she claims to have contemplated suicide, Kago bounced back, penning a book about her experiences, recording new tunes, and starring in a martial arts film with action star Sammo Hung.

Former Morning Musume member Ai Kago

COURTESY MAINSTREAM INC.

Girls *on the* Street *on music*

I came to Akiba to buy the new AKB48 DVD. **I love AKB48!**

I hate AKB48! But I love Shoko-tan!! And *seiyuu* (anime voice actors) singers.

FYI: Saya is wearing *nanchatte* (fake) uniform fashion from Eastboy

FYI: Mion is wearing *nanchatte* (fake) uniform fashion from Uniqlo

If I had the **chance to be an idol** I might give it a try.

Saya Kojima and Mion Sasaki

ANDREW LEE

The rules that made it so hard for Kago still keep budding schoolgirl idols in line today, including AKB48. And taken in the "idol" context they kind of make sense. If idols have boyfriends, what does that mean for their adoring fans? Ironically, the more real they are, the less "real" they are perceived. Perfection is an utter fabrication. The girl is human, "regular." The fantasy is dead.

Back inside the forest-green walls of the AKB48 Theater, Moeno, Rino, and Tomomi are contemplating life as idols. They may be adored by multitudes of fans, their pictures posted on bedroom walls all over the country, but they're still just girls—girls with parents, girls with teachers, girls with homework. "I am *joshi kosei*," Rino says in English mashed with the Japanese for high school girl. "It's hard to balance AKB48 and school," she adds, "but I do my homework every day." Most of their teachers know that the girls are in AKB48, and so do their classmates. But the idea that the AKB48 girls exist outside their theater—that they have a real life, and problems just like everyone else—falls under TMI (too much information) for many fans. The AKB48 theater and their homeroom class are universes apart: in one, they're expected to study and take tests, and in the other, they're exalted. "The uniform I wear to school isn't very flashy and somewhat dull," says Moeno. "But the uniforms we get to wear on stage are very colorful. I feel much happier when I'm wearing one of them."

With all those teens running around, AKB48 does seem like a girls school of sorts, and their

Other idols

IDOLS ARE NOT ONLY SINGERS. The term is also used to refer to both major or minor celebrities—who are usually in their pre-teens, teens, or twenties. Some of the non-musical idol variety include: "gravure idols" who appear in cheesecake pin-up pics, "*tarento* idols" who are TV talent, "*seiyuu* idols" who voice anime characters, and "AV idols" who do, wait for it, Adult Videos. Other more obscure idols include a train idol, a robot idol, and even a fermented bean idol.

COURTESY OFFICE 48

songs are about the angst and joys of high school—filtered through cute. Their lyrics touch on the banal, yet universal experiences

When AKB48 members **graduate from AKB48, their uniforms are re-tailored for the newest team member.**

of young love, but like Onyanko Club before it, AKB48 somehow manages to touch on controversial issues like paid dating (*enjo kosai*) while remaining pure, untarnished idols. Also like their forerunners, when the girls finish their tenure in AKB48, they graduate, or are made to graduate should something go wrong. Because for the girls in AKB48, and indeed for any idol, their careers are very much at the whim of their fans or their management. But they should be OK, for a while at least, as long as they follow the rules. ☺

AKB48 team members

The fall and rise of Rino Sashihara

EVERYTHING WAS GOING HER WAY. By early 2012, AKB48 member Rino Sashihara was starring in her own variety program, a TV drama, a feature film of said drama, and commercials, including one vegetable juice ad as a giant, laser-shooting robot. Rino Sashihara was everywhere.

Sashihara or "Sasshi" or "Sashiko," as she's affectionately dubbed, was not the cutest AKB48 member—something she often pointed out herself. But she always tried hard. Back in 2010, for example, she updated her blog 100 times in one day, netting herself 35 million page views. Sashihara's gumption made her appealing. In 2012, she rocketed to the group's forefront after being selected as AKB48's number four favorite by fans. She had yearned to be a top idol. Her dreams were coming true.

それでも
好きだよ
指原 莉乃

Rino Sashihara

Then, one of the worst things that could hit an idol happened: boyfriend allegations. Soon after AKB48's annual televised popularity contest, a Japanese tabloid published an interview with a guy claiming to be the idol's ex-boyfriend. The piece was accompanied by private, if tame, photos of Sashihara. If true, Rino Sashihara had broken one of the idol commandments: thou shall not date. Earlier that same year, two AKB48 idols had to leave the group after photos they took with guys leaked online.

The scandal hit Sashihara hard. Later, she recounted how she would start hyperventilating and couldn't keep any food down, and on AKB48's radio show she broke down crying, admitting that the guy was a friend, but denying that the whole article was true. She apologized for her behavior. Many fans were upset—one ticked-off diehard went as far as threatening to sue Sashihara for lying!

This is the part when Sashihara should have been booted out of the group, only to fade into obscurity. But she was too popular. She had a movie coming out. There were TV shows. She had proven that she could sell music. People liked her. Instead of getting the boot, she was transferred to AKB48 sister group, HKT48, on the other side of the country in Fukuoka. It might have seemed like a demotion, but it was publicity gold. The media played up the hype, with all the morning talk shows devoting time to the Sashihara scandal, and her final AKB48 concert splashed all over the daily papers. The whole thing shone the national spotlight on AKB48 and HKT48, giving the satellite group—and Sashihara—a healthy dose of free PR. The next year, she was voted as the most popular member of all the AKB48 and spin-off groups. Sashihara proved that for idols, scandals like this don't have to be career ending. They can be career making.

Sasshi's "Fortune Cookie" single

Rock'n'roll high school

Scandal

THIS FOURSOME ROSE to fame decked out like punk schoolgirls, in plaid miniskirts, cotton collared shirts, shiny neckties, and boots. Now they are everywhere: belting out their tunes on music TV shows, singing the theme songs for uber-popular anime, thrashing chords in concert halls up and down the country, their videos blasting on mega-screens on the sides of city-center buildings. Meet Haruna Ono on rhythm guitar, Mami Sazaki on bass, Tomomi Ogawa on lead guitar, and Rina Suzuki pounding the crap out of the drums. They are Scandal and they're ready to take you to planet rockula!

"When we formed the band," says guitarist and lead singer Haruna, "we wanted to learn how to put on a memorable rock show. So we rented lots of KISS videos!" As they were students when they started the band—and always rehearsed in their uniforms—their gimmick was an obvious choice over face paint. The girls also thought that wearing the same uniform wouldn't only look good on stage, but make them look like a cohesive group. They weren't acting like schoolgirls, they were schoolgirls—which had its pluses and minuses. "Being in a rock band and having to do your homework," says Rina, "was a total drag."

"Before we had the name 'Scandal'," says Tomomi, "the studio where we were practicing was on the sixth floor of a building. And every other floor was, hrmm, how should I say it? For adults?"

ALL SCANDAL IMAGES COURTESY EPIC RECORDS / SONY MUSIC

No.

TITLE

Schoolgirl
rockers
Scandal

"Shady?" says Rina.

"Sexy?" adds Haruna, while Mami cracks up.

"Sexy," continues Tomomi. "On every other floor were massage parlors. We didn't have a name, and we couldn't think of one. But one of the massage parlors was called 'Scandal', so we went with that."

The group started out paying their dues as street musicians, playing in front of Osaka Castle. "In the beginning it was really hard," admits Tomomi. Sometimes they'd play only to be ignored. Sometimes they'd play and no one was around. They printed up flyers, passed them out, and found themselves playing in clubs in Osaka and Kyoto. They were signed to an indie band label and started cutting singles, which were snapped up as soon as they hit the street. But it wasn't until after their first live show in Tokyo that they inked a major recording contract with Epic Records.

Scandal rockin' out live!

Scandal is certainly not the first girlie rock band in Japan—but in an industry where female rockers are a rarity at the top of the charts, the group stands out. "Maybe playing rock 'n' roll is embarrassing for Japanese girls," says Haruna. "Rock isn't cute. Pop is cute." For the time being, Scandal are happy to be rock 'n' rollers. Now, long graduated from high school, members have traded the school gear for an array of superstar threads. In 2012, however, Scandal held a concert at Osaka Castle Park to commemorate their start. Fittingly, the band was decked out in school uniform.

"If someone says they want to wear skirts like we did when we started out," Rina says, "then, hey, that's great. And if girls say they were inspired by us to form their own band, even better."

SCANDAL
BEST SCANDAL

Jurian Beat Crisis

"I SING SONGS about what it's like to be a school student," says fifteen-year-old Juria Kawakami. "I had my first audition when I was eleven, but I didn't get the gig," she says, "I was mortified." But, the young singer says, it was that disappointment that made her determined to be a singer. Her youthful drive seems to have paid off, making her debut as Jurian Beat Crisis (aka Juribe) on the major Japanese record label Avex in her first year of high school. With her upbeat 1980s-infused power-pop, Juribe cranks out songs full of teeny-bop angst: Her tune "Hurricane Love," for example, has Juribe smack-talking a rival girl who digs a guy she likes, while her tune "Go! Let's Go!" has her singing about her "super original" school days—the videos for both are set in school grounds and have her rocking out in uniform. Schoolgirl rock, it seems, is Big in Japan.

Juria Kawakami aka Jurian Beat Crisis

COURTESY AVEX

Girls on film

September 29, 2003. Eighteen-year-old Chiaki Kuriyama is decked out in a dark-blue school blazer, plaid skirt, and white knee-high socks. Only she isn't heading to class, she's off to the premiere of her Hollywood debut. As she graces the red carpet at Grauman's Chinese Theater, she walks up to the photographer pool, pauses, and cracks a wry smile in front of a backdrop that says Miramax Films and Coors Light. The beer maker is sponsoring the event, but it's obvious to everyone Kuriyama isn't old enough to drink. She could have chosen to wear a dress, designer jeans, anything. But there she is, in full schoolgirl mode.

>>

"I have no idea why I wore the costume to the premiere," Kuriyama says. "I guess I thought that if I didn't wear it, nobody would know who the heck I was. But if I did, I thought everybody would go, 'Ah, right, *her.*'" "Her" is Gogo Yubari, the icy-cold, sadistic, deadly ball-and-chain-wielding schoolgirl bodyguard in *Kill Bill*, Quentin Tarantino's two-volume love letter to Japanese swordplay movies, Hong Kong action cinema, and exploitation revenge flicks.

Kuriyama is chatty and polite and seemingly so well adjusted that, in light of the mess most former child actors find themselves in, it's hard to believe that the twenty-five-year-old has been in the entertainment business for two decades. Taking a break between film projects, she's sitting on a black leather sofa in her agent's office in Tokyo's fashionable Aoyama. Outside, the regal district is littered with expensive European car dealerships and boutiques. Kuriyama is petite and supermodel slender, a fashion trendsetter in her native Japan. Today she's wearing a casual black blouse and jean shorts. Half of her seems to be long, straight black hair washed with the world's greatest conditioner.

The young actress has something to confess. "Actually," she starts, putting down her tea, "I almost didn't graduate from high school

Chiaki Kuriyama as Gogo Yubari in *Kill Bill*

because of *Kill Bill*. I had too many absences." She had taken three months off to go to Los Angeles before shooting in China began. While her classmates were cloistered away studying their brains out, Kuriyama's studies were of a far more physical kind: she was training five days a week, nine 'til five, learning martial arts with the likes of Uma Thurman and David Carradine, under the tutelage of Hong Kong martial arts choreographer Wo Yu Ping. Plus, she was studying English. "I've never been very good at English," Kuriyama says. "But after being in LA for three months, I started to pick it up." Fluent or not, Kuriyama convinced her teachers that her English had improved, and she graduated from high school on schedule.

While in LA she also had a crash course in movies— an endless stream of them recommended to her by Tarantino. "Quentin showed me a lot to help explain how he saw the character," says Kuriyama. "It was during that time that the character really started to take shape in my mind." For Gogo, Tarantino wanted a tough schoolgirl to add to his gallery of brass-knuckled female characters. The director showed her the 1998 Japanese anime *Kite*, which follows Sawa, a young, exploding-bullet-firing sex-slave schoolgirl assassin whose parents are murdered. "It's very much an adult anime, but I only watched the action scenes. I love anime, but Quentin kept turning me on to anime I'd never seen before. His knowledge was amazing." Tarantino, who writes out detailed index cards on every movie he sees, was drawing on the vast reservoir of Japanese cinema he so admires. Gogo Yubari was not conjured out of thin air, but the inspiration from a long line of cinematic tough girls. Make that tough schoolgirls. Girls in sailor suits and blazers wielding weapons, ready to rumble.

© 1998,2000
YASUOMI UMETSU/
GREEN BUNNY

Sawa from the anime *Kite*

They've been making films in Japan since 1898—even right on through World War II. When the war was over, their purpose was re-calibrated from propaganda to entertainment, and in the midst of turmoil and nation rebuilding, Japanese cinema entered a golden age. *Rashomon* netted Akira Kurosawa an Academy Award for the Best Foreign Film of 1951, while later that decade the classic sci-fi monster movie *Godzilla* showed a nation still grappling with the horrific memory of the atomic bombings of Hiroshima and Nagasaki.

The 1950s also brought TV, a luxury at first, but within a decade, a living room must-have and ultimately a rival for moviegoer butts-in-seats. As audience demand grew through the 1960s and 1970s, studios needed to compete with the emerging television audience. That meant more films in color and TohoScope. But it also meant offer- ing stuff that folks couldn't see at home on TV— stuff like nudity, violence, and soft-core porn. Flicks made on the quick and cheap called *pinku eiga* (literally "pink films"), featured oodles of sex and naked flesh to keep audiences coming back for

Facing page:
Girls' Junior High School: Trouble at Graduation (1970) from Nikkatsu

more. These pink quickies started at independent studios, but the market proved too lucrative by the late 1960s for major studios to avoid. By the early 1970s, Nikkatsu, Japan's oldest movie studio, would officially enter into pink film production in the hope of lubricating its business.

Each studio had its own take on the erotic films. Nikkatsu specialized in big budget "Roman Porn" ("romance pornography") and Toei perfected the art of sadism with its "Pinky Violence" series. Since movies were shown in double features, with anti-hero yakuza flicks typically bagging top billing, the studios couldn't match some gritty, violent crime drama with, say, some happy-go-lucky musical. The bottom half of the billing either needed to be a bawdy comedy, or a pink film. Classic porn themes such as bored housewives and nubile young secretaries were common, but schoolgirls were prime exploitation fodder—and had been for decades. In the years after the war, movies about coquettish

© NIKKATSU

Girls' Junior High School: Bad Habit (1970) from Nikkatsu

bad schoolgirls, delinquent school prostitutes, and even pregnant schoolgirls were made. One of the top grossing films of 1950, the melodrama _Otome no Seine_ (_A Virgin's Sex Manual_) was promoted with the promise of a "knocked up schoolgirl." As the years passed and competition from television increased, the movies became increasingly graphic, and schoolgirls increasingly common. And for good reason; they could be depicted as submissive like in 1971's lesbian schoolgirl flick _Co-ed Report: Yuko's White Breasts_ (beware of suggestive eel use!), or horribly brutalized like in _Angel Guts: High School Co-ed_ (1978). They could also totally kick your ass. Repeatedly. That range of qualities—not to mention that they were young and cute— made Japanese schoolgirls ideal cinematic characters.

"Schoolgirls were a symbol or a metaphor," says Toshio Takasaki, a film critic who has authored multiple books on the era. "They're not meant to be real schoolgirls—they're fantasy." Takasaki believes the best way to think of these schoolgirl exploitation flicks is as parodies or homages to yakuza films. With the popularity of yakuza movies on the slide, studios were looking for something they could make on the cheap and pack with action, violence, and nudity. Schoolgirls were the answer. "Taking something very pure like a schoolgirl and putting them in an impure situation to see what happens is male reverie," Takasaki says, and the original audience was a hundred percent male. These movies were where men went to see things they could never see on TV. And oh, the things you could see!

Influenced by the American exploitation films from Roger Corman and his company American International Pictures, the flicks were sado-masochistic escapism. *Girls' Junior High School: Bad Habit*, for example, was released in November 1970 and follows dice-slinging, teacher-seducing Ryoko, who's recently relocated to Osaka from Tokyo. The school she's sent to is one tough junior high! There's brutality, including rape, and the film even touches on issues like abortion. The actresses were, of course, all of age (and looked it), but dressing them in junior high school uniforms made *Bad Habit* lurid, exploitative, and shocking. The lead actress, Junko Natsu, was actually in her twenties, but wore pigtails and a sailor uniform to help turn down the age dial. The film did well enough that two sequels, *Trouble at Graduation* and *Too Young To Play Like This*, were pumped out over the following two months.

Rival studio Toei was not to be outdone. Their *Sukeban* series show-cased the soon-to-be-legendary Reiko Ike and Miki Sugimoto playing delinquent girls who square off in a seemingly endless series of brawls, with one (or both) ending up topless. Director Noribumi Suzuki discov-ered both Ike and Sugimoto at a night club, and it was later revealed

Terrifying Girls' High School: Animal Courage (1973) from Toei

© TOEI

Terrifying Girls'
High School: Lynch
Law Classroom (1973)
from Toei

あたいらのタイマン仁義はこれだよ！

暴行、かつあげ、セックス……。
エスカレートするリンチぶりは、
まさに恐怖の女学校。

恐怖女子高校

女暴行リンチ教室

東映 成人映画

カラー作品

監督 ● 鈴木則文

杉本美樹
佐分利聖子
叶優子
太田美緒
衣麻遼子
早乙女みえ
碧川ジュリ
城恵美
一の瀬レナ
三原葉子

金子信雄
名和宏
今井健二
北村英三
井上三広

池玲子
渡瀬恒彦

映像

that the former had lied about her age to snag the role in Suzuki's *Hot Springs Mimizu Geisha*. She was only sixteen when she made her debut, causing a huge stir for appearing nude and propelling the flick to box office gold. Whether she was dishing it out in a catfight and or having it heaped on her, Ike became the iconic tough girl.

"I wanted to show the beauty and sorrow of these dark, cool, delinquent girls," says Suzuki. Now in his mid-seventies, the director and screenwriter made his mark with Pinky Violence films like the *Sukeban* and *Terrifying Girls' High School* series. His movies popularized the term sukeban, which he used after one of his staff heard it used on the street. Suzuki's *Terrifying Girls' High School* movies were just that. Terrifying. Take the opening of *Terrifying Girls' High School: Lynch Law Classroom*, the second film in the four-part-franchise. It opens in the science lab with a schoolgirl tied up. Her sailor-suit blouse is ripped open by female classmates all wearing red surgical masks, red rubber gloves, and sailor suits. They drain the poor girl's blood into flasks but she escapes, and the gang chases her up to the roof, where they rough her up until she's left hanging over the side of the building. The schoolgirl bullies step on their prey's hands, causing her to fall to her death. And that's just the opening sequence!

Terrifying Girls' High School: Women's Violent Classroom (1972) from Toei

"The movies captured the feeling of the times," Suzuki says—that turbulent time when Japan was still trying to find its place at the world's table. Intentional or not, *Lynch Law Classroom* has been seen by critics as a treatise on the campus strife of the sixties, corrupt education, immoral teachers, and bullying. Suzuki, however, disputes that there is anything deeper going on in his work, humbly stating he was a faithful Toei Studios employee, doing what his bosses wanted and making schoolgirl films for a hungry audience: "The movies I made were at the request of the company I worked for, so please don't think of them as a personal expression of my own philosophy. I was a merchant of low-brow cinema and a craftsman, free of ideology." That still does not discount the level of craftsmanship and intelligence Suzuki injected into his motion pictures.

Kinji Fukasaku was another director working around this time. During the sixties and seventies, he reinvented the yakuza genre, making _the_ organized crime flicks. What _The Godfather_ was to the New York mafia, Fukasaku's _Battles Without Honor and Humanity_ was to the yakuza. The way the characters talked, dressed, and acted have become classic, with the movie's theme becoming the signature tune for hoods

across Japan. Fukasaku went on to make a successful string of yakuza films, and continued making movies into his seventies, picking up a handful of Japanese Academy Awards for Best Picture along the way. One of his last films would deal with school children and was, as the director would later put it, a fable. A fairy tale even. From the depths of hell.

The film was _Battle Royale_ (2000), and its shocking subject matter and treatment split the country in two. Set at the turn of the millennium, the Japanese economy is in ruins, and adults, fearing student uprisings, create the Millennium Educational Reform Act. Classes of ninth-grade kids are picked for "Battle Royale," a game in which fifteen-year-olds must kill each other until only one is left standing. Wired with collars that

A scene from *Battle Royale* (2000)

detonate if they don't duke it out, the school kids are each given a weapon, which range from lethal (machine gun) to innocuous (a paper fan). Critics were sharply divided on the film and politicians criticized it as "crude," calling on the rating board for an over-fifteen rating.

"The reason why *Battle Royale* was so controversial," says Takasaki, "is that real acts of horrific school violence had recently rocked Japanese society." In 1997, a fourteen-year-old boy strangled and decapitated an eleven-year-old, putting the child's head on the gate of his school. The incident raised awareness about student-on-student violence in Japan. "Those old exploitation movies," explains Takasaki "were viewed as fantasy, but *Battle Royale* was viewed as real."

As Takasaki points out, Fukasaku's depiction of *Battle Royale* was realistic, compared to the over-the-top cartoon violence of *Kill Bill*,

Chiaki Kuriyama in *Battle Royale* (2000)

© TOEI

for example. *Kill Bill* was released in Japan without protest—despite scenes of extreme graphic violence—because it was seen as a send-up of Asian action cinema. *Battle Royale* on the other hand was viewed as a critique of the Japanese school system—where students compete against each other for coveted slots at university. For Fukasaku, *Battle Royale* was also deeply personal, and he was attracted to adapting the original book because of his own experiences working in a weapons factory as a teenager.

The director, who passed away in 2003, recounted the horrors of World War II during a retrospective at Hollywood's American Cinematique in the summer of 1997. After the ammunition factory he worked in was brutally bombed, he and the other survivors had to dispose of the mangled, severed bodies of the dead. At that moment, the fifteen-year-old Fukasaku realized everything the government had said about fighting for peace was a lie, and a lifetime of distrust of authority figures followed. "*Battle Royale*, my sixtieth film, returns irrevocably to my own adolescence," said the director in an official statement. "I had a great deal of fun working with the forty-two teenagers making this film, even though it recalled my own teenage battleground."

One of those forty-two teenagers was Chiaki Kuriyama, whose character, Takako Chigusa (aka Girl #13), proved quite adept with a knife against a male student's ballsy come-on. The powerful scene so impressed the usually dictatorial Fukasaku that it left him speechless, and it wowed Tarantino so much that the American director knew he had his Gogo. While Kuriyama might have seemed like a natural tough girl, this was virgin territory for her. "*Battle Royale* was the first action movie I ever did," Kuriyama recalls. "Before that, I'd mostly done scary movies, and my parts wouldn't get any more physical than peeking around a corner to see if the coast was clear." Kuriyama's early roles include being the victim of a horrific curse in the original straight-to-video version of *Ju-On* (*The Grudge*, 2000), made long before its Hollywood remake.

Whether it's in *Ju-On* or in dozens of other films, schoolgirls are a good-to-go stock character for Japanese horror films. In a way, they're the Japanese equivalent of sorority girls in 1980s American slasher films. They're young and cute, and a sharp contrast to the dark and sinister setting of horror films. They are also seemingly easy targets, which makes them all the more terrifying if and when they become the killers themselves. "I think the reason why there are so many schoolgirls in horror movies," suggests Kuriyama, "is that when Japanese parents don't want their kids doing bad things, they'll say, 'If you do that, a ghost or a goblin will get you.' So it makes sense to use school kids or young girls for horror movies in Japan." Scan the shelves in any Japanese video store and you'll see Kuriyama has a point—the horror section is full of films with schoolgirls being chased by goblins, ghosts, and worse.

Masato Harada's film *Suicide Song* (2007) is one of the many films on those shelves, but it is

伝
染
歌

でんせん
うた

歌えば
死ぬ。

Masato Harada's
Suicide Song
(2007)

Masato Harada's
Suicide Song
starring AKB48

© GENEON UNIVERSAL ENTERTAINMENT

hardly your typical J-horror flick. "It's kind of ridiculous that Japanese producers always want schoolgirls involved with horror," Harada says. When not directing, he teaches international relations at Nihon University, and has made movies such as 1989's post-Apocalyptic mecha-smorgasbord *Gunhed*, and 1995's guy-on-a-rampage-with-a-taxi-driver *Kamikaze Taxi*—an idea he claims Tom Cruise borrowed for *Collateral*. He also directed the plane-crash drama *Climber's High*, and acted in *The Last Samurai* and the kung-fu flick *Fearless*.

His *Suicide Song* (2007) follows a group of tabloid reporters chasing a story about schoolgirls committing suicide after singing a certain tune at karaoke. The film stars members of the idol troupe AKB48 and even includes scenes of the group performing their hit song *"Aitakatta"* at their Akihabara theater. "The AKB48 girls are normal, intelligent young women," says the director, who wanted to capture the side of their lives that has nothing to do with being idols. "They get out of school around

three-thirty and travel to Akihabara. They do that every day. And yet, they have this powerful presence on stage. That was most impressive."

While AKB48 is mentioned and shown in the flick, the dialogue between the lead actresses makes no mention of the group or of their membership. "In the movie, they're just regular schoolgirls," says Harada. As fascinated as Harada seems with the separation of school and idol, when he was offered the chance to do a picture with the idol group, he almost turned them down. "I thought, 'Oh, this is another Onyanko Club movie, and I'm not going to go through that again!'" To dispel some unpleasant memories, he needed assurance of something key: the girls' schedules.

Onyanko the Movie - Kiki Ippatsu! (1986)

© TOHO CO., LTD.

Flashback to the 1980s. The major television network Fuji TV wanted to make a feature film on über-popular idol group Onyanko Club and Harada, then a young, up-and-coming film-maker, signed on to direct. Fuji TV really ran the show, however, controlling everything. Harada says they just wanted something starring Onyanko Club to fill out the bottom billing of a double feature. The entire shoot revolved around what these schoolgirls were up to on a particular day, and the movie's production "became a slave to the girls' schedule."

Scheduling wasn't the only hurdle: casting actors proved challenging. "Onyanko Club were the ugly ducklings of the entertainment business," Harada says. It was because they were so darn amateurish, Harada points out, that the group developed a fan base, which enjoyed watching them develop as entertainers. Actors, however, were reluctant to work with these amateurish schoolgirls. "We had a hard time casting adult actors to play opposite Onyanko Club," Harada says. "Everybody hated the idea of doing a movie with them."

The director called in some favors with actor friends and was able to assemble a cast. The end result was dubbed *Onyanko the Movie—Kiki Ippatsu!* (One Shot Crisis!). Definitely not standard idol film fluff, *Kiki Ippatsu!* is *Hard Day's Night* gone horribly wrong. The story revolves around a hardcore Onyanko Club fanatic who decides he wants to kill the girls to prevent the young, cute idols from getting old and married—in a sense, to preserve their youth for eternity—and the climax has the assassin staring down Onyanko Eri Nitta in the scope of his sniper rifle. "It was kind of a risky concept," says Harada. "Whenever I write screenplays, I feel responsible to society to a certain extent. I don't want to exaggerate the delicate balance between fans and idols anymore."

Bounce koGALS (1997) by Masato Harada

More than a decade and a handful of films later, Harada made another schoolgirl related film, *Bounce koGALS*, which didn't feature idols, but *kogals*. The story follows Risa, a good schoolgirl doing bad things to get extra cash for a trip to New York. Over the course of twenty-four hours, she sells her panties, gets work on a soft-core porn video, and becomes mixed up with yakuza and unscrupulous salarymen. Risa befriends Raku and Jonko, two other schoolgirls, and the trio trick men into *enjo kosai* (paying for dates). But instead of putting out, the gals stun-gun their johns and swipe their wallets.

"They were not prostitutes," says Harada, "but very clever crooks, challenging Japan's male-dominated society." They challenged that society by playing with, and preying upon, the desires of men for profit and plunder.

Love & Pop (1998) from Hideaki Anno

Bounce koGALS was filmed in 1997, about five years after the kogals initially took to the Shibuya streets. "That first generation of kogals were rebels—rebels against the social system in Japan," Harada says. "In their own way they fought against society, and I sympathize with them for that." The film is a document of the times, realistic and natural, written in schoolgirl slang and wearing loose socks.

The movie showed that Japanese society had been turned on its ear: goody-two-shoes could be bad, and even low-lifes could be good. Kids were acting like adults, adults were acting like kids, and absolutely nothing was what it seemed.

Like *Bounce koGALS*, 1998's *Love & Pop* deals with enjo kosai. During a hot July in 1997, four loose-socks-wearing schoolgirls spend their time taking pictures, gabbing, and going on pricey paid dates. There's no sex, and the girls are earning easy money by providing dinner companionship for lonely men—that is, until one of the girls, Hiromi, spots a pricey topaz ring and delves deeper into the dating scene, much like Lisa in *Bounce koGALS*. Money and materialism propel the film forward, driving the action. The film captures the enjo kosai scene in Tokyo during the nineties with a gritty—if not sometimes, dizzying—realism.

Directed by Hideaki Anno, best known for his anime *Neon Genesis Evangelion*, and adapted from the Ryu Murakami novel *Topaz II*, *Love & Pop* was shot in the cinema verite style, using handheld digital cameras often outfitted with fish-eye lenses. The camera angles range from fetishistic (in girls' skirts or up them) to the bizarre (under a plate of spaghetti). While researching the novel that the movie is based on, Murakami interviewed schoolgirls and visited sex clubs where schoolgirls left voice mail messages trawling for clients.

Neither *Bounce koGALS* nor *Love & Pop* are typical coming of age films—the girls already act like miniature adults. Rather, the films are critiques on Japanese society, good-girls-gone-bad movies in which young women navigate a chauvinistic society. They get in over their heads, bad goes to worse and then they need to find a way out, a way to survive.

This perception of the Japanese schoolgirl has also found its way into the global imagination—if the 2006 Hollywood production of *Babel* is an example. Directed by Alejandro González Iñárritu, *Babel* features the

Rinko Kikuchi
in *Babel*
(2006)

carnal awakening of a frustrated deaf-mute sixteen-year-old schoolgirl, played by the then twenty-five-year-old Rinko Kikuchi (nominated for an Oscar for the part). In *Babel*, Kikuchi's character didn't necessarily *have* to be a schoolgirl, like she had to be deaf-mute. She could have been a college student for example. But, even in the West, loose-sock–wearing schoolgirls have been coded as sexual—and a kogal-like schoolgirl was an ideal vessel for the character's emerging desires. This was Hollywood's take on Japanese schoolgirl sexuality—cell phones, loose socks, and all. But given the fickleness and quick development of Japanese schoolgirl trends, the image can sometimes backfire.

❦ ❦ ❦

Chiaki Kuriyama has finished her ice tea and moisture collects on the side of the glass. "Originally, Gogo was going to wear loose socks," she says. "I ended up wearing regular white, knee-high socks, but the film's costume designer, who was Japanese, had prepared loose socks for me. However, Quentin went, 'Huh? Schoolgirls these days don't even wear loose socks.' Everyone was like, how did he know?" Kuriyama says, laughing. Tarantino was dead right: by 2002–2003, schoolgirls had moved on. "You know, though, when I wore Gogo's uniform," Kuriyama says. "I wore it like a real school uniform. I was a schoolgirl then. I wasn't conscious of it being a character's costume." ❦

Chiaki Kuriyama
as Gogo Yubari
in *Kill Bill*

The cult of schoolgirls

DURING THE LATE 1990s and dawn of the twenty-first century there was a B-movie renaissance of sorts with a spate of exploitation flicks that hark back to those balls-to-the-wall schoolgirl movies of the early seventies. These mixed violence, nudity and, of course, schoolgirls. Films like gore-heavy gothic horror extravaganza *Eko Eko Azarak: Wizard of Darkness* (1995), which has a sailor-suit–wearing schoolgirl-witch battling Satanic pagans in the halls of a high school. Or 2001's schoolgirl zombie film *Stacy* in which *shojo* (young girls) between the ages of fifteen and seventeen turn into brain-dead, flesh-eating gals called Stacies. The only way to stop these zombie schoolgirls is to cut them into pieces, so cue the bunny chainsaw girls and the *Evil Dead* homages!

These films were made by a generation of directors who came of age watching flicks from Japan's heyday of exploitation. "I was really influenced by Japanese action and horror films of the 1970s," says filmmaker Noburo Iguchi, who cut his teeth doing schoolgirl-themed porn in the nineties. "The reason why you see so many schoolgirl-types in Japanese adult videos," he says, "is that the uniform costume itself is a vessel for male fantasies about female purity." It's not simply the baby-faced girl that's getting viewers off, in other words, but the article of clothing she wears.

Iguchi's "mainstream" non-porn releases include 2008's *The Machine Girl*. The picture is standard revenge film

Minase Yashiro is *The Machine Girl*

From the Creators of "Death Trance" and "Meatball Machine"

It's Payback Time!

A TOKYO SHOCK ORIGINAL

THE **MACHINE** GIRL

吸血少女対少女フランケン
Vampire Girl vs Frankenstein Girl

Vampire Girl vs Frankenstein Girl (2009)

fare—heroine is wronged and seeks her vengeance—but the violence is pure shlock horror. The "machine girl" of the title is Ami, a schoolgirl who stands up to bullies, only to learn that they're ninja bullies! She comes out of the fight minus most of an arm, but soon has a Gatling gun attached to her stump by a friendly mechanic, and unleashes her fury with an interminable spray of bullets.

The Machine Girl has developed a cult following outside its native Japan, and has even had an American theatrical release. "I was truly surprised that a film that was overlooked in Japan could get noticed abroad—especially with the inherent cultural differences," Iguchi says. "It's inspiring." He was inspired enough, it seems, to follow *The Machine Girl* with a bashful sequel called *Shyness Machine Girl*, which memorably has a schoolgirl fire a machine gun out of her butt. "I'm not striving for the real, but the surreal, " says Iguchi. "And I dig female characters in school uniforms."

The Sultan of Splatter

THEY DON'T GET MUCH BETTER than Yoshihiro Nishimura. Or grosser. When director Noburo Iguchi needed to turn a schoolgirl's arm into a Gatling gun for *The Machine Girl* or when he needed a lethal butt tentacle for *Zombie Ass*, it was special-effects master Yoshihiro Nishimura he called. Ditto for filmmaker Sono Shion when he needed fifty-four schoolgirls to jump in front of a train at Tokyo's Shinjuku Station for his film *Suicide Circle*. Nishimura's symphonies in splatter have made his work famous worldwide. The gore guru is also a director in his own right, creating bloody opuses that often feature schoolgirl characters.

Yoshihiro Nishimura

"What, you're not interested in sailor uniforms?" Nishimura jokes, noting that his films not only reflect his personal taste, but that of his largely male audience. "When the number of female horror film fans increases, I'd like to do a film with a schoolboy lead." No doubt so Nishimura can annihilate him with special effects!

But Nishimura's films not only feature schoolgirl characters, they parody youth and social trends. In his 2008 film *Tokyo Gore Police*, for example, there's a commercial for "Wrist Cutter G," a darkly humorous take on Casio's adorable Baby-G watches that were a hit with teens in the 1990s. Here, it's not wristwatches, but wrist *cutters*. During the early 2000s, the Japanese media covered the popularity of wrist cutting among masochistic teens, pointing out that the self-mutilation was an obvious cry for help and even stating that young girls did it to relieve stress. In the "Wrist Cutter G" spot, a trio of schoolgirls cavort about with colorful blades as CG bubbles float across the screen, flashing their slit wrists and chirping things like, "It doesn't hurt that much." The mix of schoolgirl cute and schoolgirl horror is unsettling, but that's the point. The ad was such a good parody of cute Japanese marketing that when a YouTube version went viral, some even wondered if this was a real commercial for a real Japanese product!

Growing up, Nishimura was interested in film—especially American horror. Through these movies, he discovered the craftsmanship behind the gore and became a fan of movie special-effects artists. According to Nishimura, "I was the kind of junior high school kid who was thinking things like, 'How did they do that decapitation scene?'" Bitten by the movie bug—the bloody movie bug—Nishimura began creating his own homemade special effects, first covering his friends in phony splatter, then starting to make his own movies. His big break came when he was hired to do the special effects for the 2001 horror flick *Suicide Circle* in which a rash of schoolgirls begin killing themselves.

Nishimura admits that pulling off the film's unforgettable opening scene, where fifty-four uniformed schoolgirls commit mass suicide at Shinjuku Station, was tricky. Not only that, the scene ended up being censored by the country's motion picture association for too much blood and guts. Working with all that gore must have been stomach-churning for Nishimura, right? Not exactly. "It's less important how the effects make me feel," says the filmmaker, "and more important how they make the audience feel."

As You Like It

A BOY PRETENDING to be a girl, who's played by a girl who's a porn actress. Confused? For soft core exploitation flick *Sukeban Boy* (*Oira Sukeban*, 2006), adult video director Noboru Iguchi roped in AV idol Asami to play Banji Suke—a tough teen dude that looks like a babe.

"Since I've started doing movies, it seems like all I've had to do was strip off," says twenty-four-year-old Asami. Not so with *Sukeban Boy*—in which she's actually trying to keep her clothes on. After Asami's character gets expelled from multiple schools—for fighting with class-mates who tease him for looking like a girl—his father convinces the lad to cross-dress in a sailor uniform and attend an all-girls school. Unfortunately his troubles aren't over, as the girls school isn't much better! There he faces gangs like the No Bra Club, the Pantyhose Club, and the Full Frontal League, who terrorize the school halls.

Men playing women is a comedy of errors. It's like Shakespeare . . . sort of. While *Sukeban Boy* was adapted from the Go Nagai manga, the inspiration for casting a woman to play a man dressing as a woman came when Iguichi noticed how effemi-nate some young Japanese male actors are. "I thought why not make a movie where the main male lead is played by a tough chick?" says the director.

The cast, mostly porn stars, hams it up as ditzy, psychotic schoolgirls, parodying the pouty, meant-to-be-arousing performances they give as schoolgirls in adult films. And in turn, show just how ridiculous it is to have a twenty-something-year-old try to pass herself off as a fifteen-year-old.

Asami (left) as *Sukeban Boy*

Noboru Iguchi's *Sukeban Boy* (2006)

© 2006 GO NAGAI DYNAMIC PRODUCTIONS/KINGRECORDS

© 2006 GO NAGAI DYNAMIC PRODUCTIONS/KINGRECORDS

Girls on the Street on movies

I like **action movies**!

I like **Japanese movies**, basically any movie my favorite actor is in! And I want to see that new Disney movie!

But I prefer **TV**.

The schoolgirls in Japanese TV dramas and movies are **extremely cute**!

Mei Hiraoka and Shiori Matsui

ANDREW LEE

Material girls

Lines of girls. Endless, endless girls. The queue of cute wraps around the National Gymnasium in Yoyogi, Tokyo, as the hot afternoon sun beats down on the cobblestoned pavement. It's hardly ideal terrain for stiletto heels, but none of the girls seem to care. And if they do, they're sure not showing it. This is where the 1964 Olympics' swimming and diving events were held, yet it's not a sporting event the girls are waiting for. That is, unless you consider fashion a sport. These young women are lined up for the Tokyo Girls Collection (TGC), an event unlike anywhere else on earth.   >>

The queue waiting to get into Tokyo Girls Collection

PICTURES ANDREW LEE

More of a fashion festival than a fashion show, and bigger in size and scope than Tokyo Fashion Week, TGC has been held twice a year since August 2005. Unlike the haute couture seen on the runways of Milan, Paris, New York, and London, this is accessible fashion, clothes you can actually buy, along with new products to test, sample, and take home.

At the front of the twenty-three thousand people patiently waiting to get in, stands an eighteen-year-old girl and her buddies. They've been there for twelve hours, since one in the morning. A couple of hundred feet behind them is a young man who was dragged all the way from Beijing by his girlfriend specifically for the event. Even further back in the queue two uniformed schoolgirls join the line as the doors open and the line pushes forward. Beautifully.

Backstage preparation is in full swing. The heavy smell of perfume hangs in the air, and staffers with megaphones scurry about, telling the models to get ready. Foundation, lipstick, eye shadow, and other

Schoolgirl
fans of
TGC

The crowd inside
the National
Gymnasium

cosmetics are laid out on rows of makeshift picnic tables. One table
holds a mountain of blow driers. Three women in surgical masks massage the feet of models sprawled out on sofas. One of the girls, in a leop-
ard print jacket, is chewing someone out on the phone as her limbs get a
good work over. Not far away are two lines of duct tape on the floor
where other girls are practicing their runway struts. "Legs up, legs up!"
barks the show's choreographer.

"I think the Tokyo Girls Collection really shows the power that young
girls have," says Marie, a half-Japanese, half-Canadian girl who is a well
known model-turned-TV-star. "This is more than a fashion show, and it
reflects the reality of Japanese fashion way better than Tokyo Fashion
Week," she adds. "These are clothes girls can actually buy *while* we're
modeling them." And this is what makes TGC so groundbreaking.

Here's how it works: using their mobile phones, attendees register
online via the GirlsWalker.com portal. Then, during the event, they can

watch the fashion being modeled on the runway and simultaneously toggle through the same clothes on their phone's screen. If they like what they see, they can purchase the clothes then and there by credit card, transfer from a bank account, or even pay cash-on-delivery—all arranged via mobile phone. If they don't want to shop online, girls can visit the brands' stores later where signs point out which outfits were worn on the TGC runway.

Tokyo Girls Collection is at the intersection of fashion, technology, hyper consumerism, and brilliant marketing. Rampant capitalism, ready to serve these girls, and give them exactly what they want. It offers a huge number of young women the chance to experience a world that usually only exists on the pages of glossy magazines. Here they can see their favorite models and TV talent up—relatively—close. The main stage is a fashion runway that juts 130 feet out into the sea of young, dolled up, excited girls. Once the models start to emerge the crowd is going to go nuts. The show's choreographer, Fumihito, sums up the atmosphere best. "In Japan, these models are like idols. Girls worship them."

Cute fashion at TGC

Show attendees shell out between 5,000 and 7,000 yen for tickets (about US$70), but they get more than the fashion parades. There are acts by popular singers, and booths surround the runway

PICTURES COURTESY TGC

Models and their adoring fans at TGC

pushing cosmetics and clothing companies' latest products. There's a candy company handing out mobile-phone straps advertising their chewing-gum. A soup company is giving away instant soup. Even Toyota bows before the power of this audience with a display for its latest compact car. "The Tokyo Girls Collection is a huge draw for young women," says the Toyota booth staffer.

Cosmetics maker Pias is passing out tubes of a not-yet-launched version of its mascara. "The girls who come to Tokyo Girls Collection are incredibly fashion conscious and interested in make-up," says company spokesperson Ayako Sato. It's the first time Pias has set up a TGC booth, mixing promotion with market research. Those hoping to get samples either need to fill out surveys or register their contact info. It's not just domestic companies either—Maybelline New York has a booth. "There really aren't that many events where you get a turnout of 20,000 young women," says Maybelline's Junko Mizobuchi. That's a lot of potential customers ready and willing to try and, perhaps, buy the latest products.

The lights dim and smoke machines go into action. With the whole joint packed with woman in their mid-teens to mid-twenties, you could cut the estrogen with knife. A woman's voice suddenly blares out of huge speakers and in American-accented English says, "It all started four years ago with the blinking light of a mobile phone." A computer graphic of a mobile phone appears on three huge screens and the voice proclaims dramatically "Let Japan's real clothes go global!" On screen a 24-style digital clock begins the countdown.

The mobile phone revolution came early to gadget-crazy Japan, and 80 percent of Japanese now own at least one. There are over 100 million users with advanced third generation handsets. But it was schoolgirls, not business men, who kicked phone technology into high gear. And it all started with pagers.

Originally intended for salary men, pagers caught on with teens in the early nineties, and millions and millions of colorful versions called "Pocket Bell" were sold. Professor Mizuko Ito, a cultural anthropologist known for her research on how teens use technology, suggests that Pocket Bells were the first viral youth tech. Though basically just a pager, what made the Pocket Bell different was how teens starting using them. Instead of punching in a phone number for a call back, kids started sending each other primitive messages using numbers. The coded patterns varied from school to school, and friend to friend, but by

Paging Japanese schoolgirls . . .

What codes did schoolgirls send to their friend's pagers?

3341   *samishii* (I'm lonely). Three (3) being read as *san* or *mitsu*, four (4) as *shi*, and one (1) as *i*.

106410   *teru shite* (Telephone me). Ten (10) can be *tou* or even *dou*, but here it is *te*, because it's short for "ten." Six (6) is *ru* for six *roku*. Four (4) is once again *shi* and again ten (10) is *te*.

14106   *ai shiteru* (I love you). One (1) meaning *ai* as the number one looks like the letter "i." Four (4) is *shi*, ten (10) is *te* and six (6) is *ru*.

When pagers evolved to display more than numbers pressing the number **"1" twice** would create the Japanese character あ. Pressing **"2"** then **"1"** would create the Japanese character か, while pressing **"3" then "1"** would create さ, and so on.

RC-101

POCKET BELL

NTT

NTT DOCOMO

The Pocket Bell from NTT

using them, girls could trans-mit secret messages right under the noses of nosey parents and school authorities.

"What makes the case of the Pocket Bell so unique," says Ito, "was how quickly the industry acted." Mobile service providers responded to the potential in the teen market by rolling out models in various colors. More importantly, they introduced a simple text message function. Instead of primitive numeric codes, characters from the Japanese alphabet could be input by punching in certain combinations of numbers. It was the start of text messaging: anyone could phoneti-cally write Japanese using these number combinations. Seeing girls quickly punching out text messages on public pay phones was a common sight by the mid-1990s, and this kind of mobile communication soon filtered through the rest of society. It was an effect Ito calls "trick up phenomenon," and it ultimately led to the multifunctional mobile phones that flood the market today.

The first shots of the mobile phone revolution were fired in 1994 when regulations were changed to make it easier to buy mobile phones, rather than renting them. Two years later, phone carrier NTT DoCoMo released the first Personal Handy-phone System (PHS) which, unlike cellular phones, was restricted to urban areas and domestic calls. The smaller radius of phone coverage was no problem for someone trying to get in touch with buddies from class! Less coverage also meant a lower price, and a lower price, in turn, meant schoolgirls could afford the handsets—or get their parents to buy them. While not specifically designed for schoolgirls, it was a perfect fit for their social butterfly needs. "The mobile phone was revolutionary," says Ito. "Until then teens couldn't really talk that much to each other in class and their parents monitored the landline at home. The mobile phone enabled them to finally have private conversations."

The mobile phone, known in Japan as a *keitai* or *keitai denwa* (literally "portable phone"), is a private device, especially in Japan where people use it more for texting than talking. The shape itself makes it intimate because it fits in the pad of the hand. "Teens changed the mobile phone demographic from a business demographic that needed portable phones in order to be reachable for work," says Ito, "to an everyone demographic." For teens looking for some semblance of privacy in the cramped houses they shared with their parents, the mobile phone was a godsend. It not only offered privacy, but mobility, making it possible to be connected with friends 24–7.

New features were introduced in response to what was happening on the street. Sharp, for example, released the first keitai with built-in digital camera to capitalize on the schoolgirl photo craze and sticker picture

ANDREW LEE

For Japanese teens, the mobile phone was revolutionary

boom of the late 1990s. And when digital snaps proved to be a hit, companies created small printers for mobile phone pics and even kiosks where kids could print out phone photos.

In 1999, NTT DoCoMo launched iMode, which brought the internet and email to the mobile phone. Email made it possible to send longer messages than the limited character texting of the time, and schoolgirls, of course, were the first to respond. And where they led, others followed. "In the late nineties," Ito says, "text messaging was associated with girls' culture. But it spread from there." Though men were

GirlsWalker.com and TGC websites

ANDREW LEE

originally hesitant to use text messaging because it had such a strong schoolgirl connotation, it is now indispensable across the spectrum of users. However, it is still girls that fuel its use—according to Ito's data 100 percent of middle and high school girls who own mobile phones use email. It is schoolgirls Japan has to thank for the proliferation of mobile phones, and for the many now standard functions—especially for the spread of the mobile phone-based internet.

With so many young shopping-mad women tied to their mobile phones, tech-savvy retailers began to push chic boutiques through handset-based websites. While the PC internet is largely dominated by male users in Japan, the mobile internet has long been a female refuge of sorts, with young Japanese women more likely to access the internet through their handsets than a computer. A company called Mavael even released a computer keyboard, called the "Keiboard," that was shaped like a mobile phone in the vain hope of aiding the migration from mobile to personal computer. Other companies like Branding, the company behind the Tokyo Girls Collection, realized that the keitai is where it's at—and launched GirlsWalker.com in summer 2000. Branding's data shows that in 2008, 65 percent of girls between their high teens and early twenties shopped online via their mobile phones. Their

GirlsWalker.com site features fashion from Shibuya's hottest shops—allowing girls from across the country to buy the latest fashions through their phone. In short, the site brings city trends to fashion conscious girls stuck in the sticks.

A year after GirlsWalker.com launched, sales on the site had quadrupled, and it became Japan's number one mobile phone portal-site. GirlsWalker didn't stop there, spreading beyond the internet to become a brand name—a "Good Housekeeping Seal of Approval" of sorts—that is stamped on "healthy" convenience store food and drinks targeted at young women. There are even GirlsWalker.com branded vending machines, stocked full of beverages designed to appeal to girls. And don't forget, of course, there's the Tokyo Girls Collection itself.

ॐ ॐ ॐ

A couple of weeks before TGC, Shinji Takenaga, the president of Shibuya-based market research firm ING, sits in the company's meeting room. He's wearing a red Tommy Hilfiger polo shirt and designer jeans that belie his forty years of age. Takenaga's relaxed manner of speech and chilled attitude suit his youthful working environment—the next room is filled with schoolgirls.

Schoolgirls hard at work in the offices of ING

ANDREW LEE

"Schoolgirls are the hardest market," he says. "Because they're the hardest to predict. Nobody knows what they're going to do next." If anyone would know that nobody knows what schoolgirls are going to do next, it's Takenaga, whose firm specializes in their trends and tastes. "If Japanese companies would just listen to these schoolgirls, and deliver what they say they want," says Takenaga, "they might not get a surefire hit, because there are no surefire hits. But they wouldn't get a flop."

This is the philosophy behind Takenaga's company, which has about 1,500 schoolgirls between the ages of fifteen and eighteen registered in Tokyo alone. ING also has branches in Nagoya and Osaka. "If girls have a part-time job at McDonalds or a convenience store, they have to work regular shifts," Takenaga says. "At ING, we don't have regular shifts—we simply tell girls when there's a focus group or other event. They have the freedom to work whenever they want, and to decide what it is they want to do. Another major difference from regular part-time work is that here their opinion means something." In fact, companies pay good money to hear what they have to say. ING's clients are both foreign and domestic, and include cosmetics, music, mobile phone, and internet companies who all want to know what makes these

ING president Shinji Takenaga with some of his helpers

girls tick. They have good reason to. When schoolgirls buy something in Japan, they buy it in a big way.

To test if something is cool on the street and in school, ING enlists girls in buzz campaigns, giving them free samples to pass out to their friends and to get feedback. "Some have the assumption that if we just give the girls samples it will create a buzz," says Takenaga. "But it doesn't work like that." The girls are arbiters of taste, and if they dig a particular product, then they will tell their friends, and their friends will tell their friends, and a whole daisy chain is created. It's a multiplier, compounded by the fact that the girls have money to burn. Nearly 80 percent of schoolgirls have their parents pay their phone bills, and according to ING polling, nearly 40 percent of them carry over seven thousand yen at any time, with 22 percent carrying more than ten thousand yen. When you're living at home with mom and dad, that's totally disposable income to shell out and shop, shop, shop. And where better to shop than in Shibuya?

Tokyo's Shibuya district is Japan's youth mecca and ground zero for schoolgirls. "The reason why there are so many schoolgirls in Shibuya is 109," says Takenaga. The 109 building, or simply *ichi-maru-kyu* (one-oh-nine) as the kids call it, is an eight-story cylindrical shopping building that represents all that is trendy, cute, and cool about Shibuya.

A typical focus group at ING

PICTURE ANDREW LEE

The iconic
Shibuya 109
building

ANDREW LEE

When 109 initially threw open its doors in 1979, it wasn't targeting teens, but women in their late twenties and thirties fueled by the Bubble Economy—the economic "miracle" of the post-war era. But when the Japanese economy imploded during the stagnant 1990s, schoolgirls' carefree shopping kept on keeping on, while the purse strings of adults tightened. With pocket change from parents, part-time jobs, and doting relatives, young girls had money when

Shibuya Crossing

ANDREW LEE

no one else did. Adult spending in Shibuya was replaced by schoolgirl spending. More karaoke parlors and teen-geared clothing shops opened in the area and the number of stores targeting teens in 109 exploded. By 1996 its designation as a teen haven was made official with a renovation of the building. One-oh-nine became the epicenter for a teen fashion quake that shook Japan, and schoolgirls were suddenly a bright spot in the country's abysmal economy, powering big-selling trends.

Take, for example, Tamagotchi, the game featuring virtual pets that owners had to feed and take care of. The toy was launched in late 1996 and sold tens of millions of units in Japan thanks, in big part, to the buzz among schoolgirls. They became a national, and then international, craze.

Tamagotchi from Bandai

© BANDAI 1996

GAME LASVEGAS
プリクラのメッカ

ANDREW LEE

Purikura Mecca in Shibuya

Sticker pictures from Furyu

Around the same time, rows of schoolgirls were lining up in front of arcades to have their pictures taken by sticker picture machines, (think photo booth, but with cute, color pix printed out on sticky paper.) The machines, called *Print Club* (or *Purikura*), were released by the game developer Atlus and were initially aimed at salarymen who could take their photo and get a sticker to put on their business card. But when schoolgirls discovered the machines, they were head over heels in love. Other companies like Konami, Taito, and Namco began making their own machines, adding features in response to what girls wanted. Once again schoolgirls had found something, made it their own, and turned it into a smash hit. And once again, they were telling a nation what was cool and what wasn't.

But just as they can make a product, schoolgirls can break a product, and break it bad. For example, when their attention to the Tamagotchi eventually wandered elsewhere, toy maker Bandai was left with a stock pile of 2.5 million unsold Tamagotchi and losses of US$66.8 million. And in another case—reported in the *Financial Times*—when British telecom giant Vodafone tried its hand at the Japanese market by buying a controlling interest in J-Phone, the company's failure to respond to the wants and needs of Japanese schoolgirls cost Vodafone its market share. Those schoolgirls who signed up when J-Phone introduced camera phones jumped ship because of spotty signal reception

Girls on the Street on shopping

109 is full of gyaru!

It's got seriously cute clothes and always has the latest trends, but it's a bit expensive!

But having so many brands together is good!

SHIBUYA 109

Loose socks: back in fashion in 2010!

If I shop alone I can go at my own pace, but it's more fun with friends!

I help my mom choose her clothes!

I shop with my friends because we share the same sense of style

Fuuka Ishi, Ruriko Kudou, and Momoka Suyama

ANDREW LEE

and sluggish text service. It got so bad that Vodafone sold its controlling interest to a domestic telecom. While often found in other global markets, this kind of boom-bust is amplified in the world of the schoolgirl.

☼ ☼ ☼

After more than six hours of pure fashion indulgence the spotlights finally go dim at the Tokyo Girls Collection. Thousands of girls flood out onto the dark streets of Harajuku, pouring down into Shibuya, the belly of the beast. Carrying their bags of free TGC goodies, the girls head home, past the shuttered doors of endless boutiques. The last train may be calling, but mobile phones are only a flip open away. In the twenty-four hours surrounding the event, the equivalent of more than $650,000 in clothing and goods will be sold through event booths and TGC mobile phone and computer websites. And there's always more shopping left to be done, still so many cute, cool things left to buy. ☺

TGC wraps up for another season

Charisma clerks

THEY'RE NOT JUST CLERKS—they're *charisma* clerks! During the late 1990s when schoolgirls were on a spending frenzy, Shibuya 109 boutiques like Egoist began racking up big sales numbers thanks in part to their go-getter salesgirls.

Former charisma clerk Yoco Morimoto

These "charisma clerks" did not use the sometimes stiff and overly polite customer-clerk relationship traditionally found in Japanese retail settings. They were hired because they were fashion leaders in their own right and could offer friendly, casual advice on clothes to clientele. They weren't just peddling to customers, they were like buddies, masters of the soft sell. Take charisma-clerk-turned-fashion-mogul Yoco Morimoto, who once sold over 1 million yen (over US$10,000) worth of threads in the course of one hour.

"The term 'charisma clerk' is just something created by the media," says Morimoto, who worked at Egoist's 109 shop. "Back then, various magazine editors would wander around 109, looking for salespeople to interview, and that's how they found me." Fellow Egoist salesgirl Reiko Nakane says she was simply listening to the needs of the customers. "I didn't even know what a charisma clerk was until I was called one."

Whether charisma clerks were simply created by the media to sell magazines or not, these girls did have charisma—moxy, even! Yoco Morimoto went on to advise the fashion line Moussy and is now a successful brand producer for Japanese fashion label KariAng. Nakane is the creative director for the oh-so-cool girl's brand rienda. Not all the charisma clerks went on to such fashionable heights, but for a generation of schoolgirls, they redefined the way clothes are bought and sold in Japan.

Kawaii kulture

SCHOOLGIRLS SAY IT. Little kids say it. Even men, *gasp*, say it. Anywhere you go in Japan, you will hear it said, if not squealed: "*kawaii*." It basically means "cute," but also carries connotations of adorable, precious, and charming. It is convenient for meaningless compliments and is often overused. Kawaii can describe just about anything and when kawaii alone won't do, things can be *kimokawaii* (creepy cute), *erokawaii* (sexy cute), or *busukawaii* (ugly cute). The bar for cute is much lower than the more serious *utsukushii* (beautiful). Kawaii is light and fluffy. It's ambiguous, personal, individual, and doesn't have to conform to clearly defined concepts of Japanese beauty. Beauty is natural, but kawaii can be manufactured. And it's attainable—any girl can be cute.

Even Hello Kitty has been known to wear loose socks

"Kawaii" has long been used to refer to babies and animals much like "cute" in English. But during the 1970s, the word began to sneak into the female lexicon. At the time, character goods like Snoopy bags were popular with teenagers, who might have never read *Peanuts*, but simply dug the way the beagle looked. Superficial maybe, however, this ability to accept images without knowing their original context underscores a Japanese propensity to absorb foreign culture based simply on visual cues found appealing.

In 1975 the character most closely associated with Japanese cute was launched when the Sanrio character goods company released a snap-top coin purse featuring the now iconic Hello Kitty or "Kitty-chan" as she's affectionately known in Japan. The big-headed cat, with her trademark red bow, sat between a gold fish bowl and a milk bottle. The story Sanrio created had her hailing from London and bearing the English name Kitty White. She oozed cute.

© 1976, 2010 SANRIO CO., LTD.

As the obsession for all things kawaii exploded in the late seventies and early eighties, Sanrio stuck the cat's mug on stationery goods, coinciding with a trend in which girls deliberately made their handwriting look like it was written by a young child because they believed it was kawaii. Increasingly, the meaning of "kawaii" began to blur. If a Hello Kitty bag was called "kawaii," did that mean the bag itself was cute? Or the character? Or the combination of both? As Kitty-chan's popularity grew, her face could be found on everything from stuffed animals and posters to waffle irons and somewhat dubious massage wands.

Some critics have pinned the Japanese fascination with cute to the infantilization of society after the country's defeat in World War II. However this is a gross oversimplification that assumes that Japanese concepts of cute began when the war ended. It also overlooks the impact of Western imports like Disney on manga, and discounts universal feelings of childhood nostalgia. But cute things are bought by young Japanese women for the same reason LEGO or a model train may be bought by an adult Western man, and for the same reason that grown Japanese men and women find schoolgirls so appealing: they represent being young. At its very core, kawaii captures both the nostalgic memories of days gone by and the adoration of youth's sparkle. Schoolgirls are the physical embodiment of that concept, while Hello Kitty is the commercialization of it.

The Japanese girls who grew up in the kawaii boom of the 1970s didn't abandon all things pink and fluffy when they became adults. As they became mothers their children were likewise bred on a diet of cute, and kawaii culture seeped into the national consciousness, one generation after the next. Not everything in Japan is cute, but it is one way in which Japan likes to represent itself to the outside world. Besides already being a UNICEF envoy, Hello Kitty was named Japan's official Tourism Ambassador by the Japanese government in 2008.

The original Hello Kitty coin purse from 1975

The Kawaii Manifesto

HEAD DOWN THE FASHIONABLE BACK STREETS of Tokyo's Harajuku, and you'll find it: a pink three-story building. Take the stairs up to the second floor, and if the fuchsia facade wasn't enough of a visual assault, take a step inside. The pastel colors are overwhelming—the yellows, the baby blues, and, of course, the endless pinks. It's a visual sugar high that looks more like a box of candy than a clothing store. Adorable outfits hang throughout, a merry-go-round pony smiles in the window, and cute American plush toys—like Care Bears, My Little Pony, and Popples—live on the shelves. Welcome to sensational lovely world! Welcome to 6%DokiDoki.

This world-famous clothing boutique isn't simply "kawaii" or "cute." Oh no, this iconic shop is "sensational kawaii." And for 6%DokiDoki's mastermind, Sebastian Masuda, the original Japanese word "kawaii" (可愛い) is a delicate, complex, and nuanced word. "If you translate 'kawaii' into English, it's 'cute,' but kawaii is more emotional than cute," explains Masuda. And 6%DokiDoki is much more than a clothing store. And Sebastian Masuda is more than a fashion mogul. His background is theater and contemporary art—both of which served as an inspiration for 6%DokiDoki. "I wanted to create something that was not a one time performance, but a place where that performance could continue daily," said Masuda. The result was 6%DokiDoki. In Japanese, "dokidoki" refers to the throbbing of a heart, or excitement. "I wanted to convey the meaning that this store stocked merchandise that was just a little dokidoki," says Masuda. "So I went with 6 percent."

6% DokiDoki

The shop opened in 1995, specializing in the kawaii and the colorful as well as the unusual, such as bug-collecting containers sold as bags and traditional Japanese shop-entrance curtains made into hair accessories. While the key concept was "kawaii," some of the store's biggest inspirations for its unique look weren't Japanese.

While on a trip to LA, Masuda discovered My Little Pony and Popples—which, at the time, were "totally not popular," Masuda points out. He was blown away by them and bought as many as he could find. "They're cute and colorful, but they are also a little creepy and seem to have an edge which makes them kawaii, yet not kawaii," says Masuda. For him, that interplay of adorable and slightly unsettling is what kawaii is all about. This contrast proved to be a hit: after Sofia Coppola sang the store's praises in 1996, Masuda recalls that more celebs started showing up and suddenly Japanese fashion mags started running articles and photo spreads on the shop. 6%DokiDoki might have only offered 6 percent excitement, but the buzz around the store was well over the 100 mark. Masuda and 6%DokiDoki

"PonPonPon"
Kyary
Pamyu Pamyu

WARNER MUSIC JAPAN 2011, COURTESY 6%DOKIDOKI

became the fashion and style leaders for the day-glow crowd in Harajuku.

The store's visual pyrotechnics are no accident. When Masuda was seven, he suddenly lost his hearing. "I had to compensate with my sense of sight to figure out what was going on around me," says Masuda. "I think that made me more observant than typical people." But it wasn't only that: after his hearing returned, Masuda became increasingly perceptive and sensitive to sound. This heightened perception has led him to try and express sound through visual presentation.

Masuda has taken his visual sense to the masses, directing music videos and doing 6%DokiDoki fashion shows across the globe. In 2012, he directed Kyary Pamyu Pamyu's "PonPonPon" music video, which featured Pamyu Pamyu, a 6%DokiDoki customer and former schoolgirl fashion blogger, singing and dancing in a room cluttered with colorful stuffed animals and clothes, a huge box of Kraft Macaroni & Cheese, and floating brains and eyeballs. "Usually, my work focuses on the space between girl's wild delusions and reality," says Masuda, "but for the 'PonPonPon' video, the concept was 'a girl who doesn't tidy her room.'" This wasn't just some high-concept music video, however, this was Masuda's artistic statement on kawaii—the interplay between the adorable and the unsettling, between the cute and the creepy. "For me," says Masuda, "'kawaii' is a place you create, a small universe that reflects your own world view and where you can make your own happiness."

Bringing Harajuku to the world

STEP INTO 6% DOKIDOKI'S HARAJUKU STORE and you'll see her. But Yuka is more than just a sales clerk—she's a "charisma clerk" whose job it is to be the face of the brand, giving guidance and inspiration to customers who aspire to be part of Harajuku's colorful, cute, and sometimes outrageous fashion culture. Yuka is a Harajuku emissary.

When Sebastian Masuda travels the globe to show off 6%DokiDoki's "sensational kawaii" stylings, she comes along, showing just how sensationally cute 6%DokiDoki can be. "I'm thrilled we can convey the spirit of Harajuku in far away places," says Yuka.

The clothes are flashy—a far cry from traditional Japanese fashion and even more traditional Japanese school uniforms— hence the allure. "I was a huge fan of 6% DokiDoki while in high school," Yuka gushes. After graduating high school, Yuka, now in her early twenties, started working at the Harajuku store.

"School rules say that everybody has to wear the same uniform, so it's hard to express yourself," says Yuka. "And that's why there's a longing for liberated fashion." If uniform fashion is expressing yourself within a set of rules, then 6%DokiDoki is breaking all of them in the most kawaii way possible.

Yuka— charisma clerk

COURTESY 6% DOKIDOKI

Hot Japanese schoolgirls!

UNBRIDLED SPENDING and trend-setting has turned the Japanese schoolgirl into such an icon of consumerism that companies even use their image to sell things. "Japanese schoolgirls are a brand," says market researcher Shinji Takenaga, "and they know it." Turn on the TV, or flip through a magazine, and there they are: schoolgirls in their short plaid skirts, running on a beach, or sitting on a park bench. The goods they hawk include chocolate snacks, ice cream, sports drinks, mobile phones, and even insurance. "Keep in mind, no one actually buys products because schoolgirls appear in the ads," contests Takenaga. "Schoolgirls aren't endorsing a product, but rather, they're happy, cheerful, cute characters." That help things sell.

Hokubi Foods' "High School Girl" brand kimchi

In 1999, the Itoh Ham food company actually registered the words for "High School Girl" (*Joshi Kosei*) as a trademark to use for a line of healthy food products. Nothing says delicious ham like a schoolgirl—or something? A Hiroshima company did one better and released "High School Girl Kimchi," spicy Korean pickles branded with co-eds.

What's the schoolgirl connection with a Korean side dish? "My company was launching its brand of kimchi so late," says Hokubi Foods president Etsuko Matsumori, "that we needed a name people would remember." When the product launched roughly half of the customers, Matsumori estimates, bought the schoolgirl kimchi simply because they thought it was interesting. But the schoolgirl image was chosen for a reason. "A lot of women want to go back to that period when they were cute schoolgirls," says Matsumori. "They want to get that feeling about being willing to try anything." Schoolgirl kimchi, for instance.

When companies don't secure big name actors or singers it seems schoolgirls are the default product pitchperson. They can appeal to both men and women, young and old alike. A teen in a sailor suit or a plaid skirt is cute, young, healthy, happy, and has a future of endless possibilities. They are branded as perfect, and are, in turn, the perfect brand.

Trends fueled by schoolgirls

Hello Kitty: Known in Japan as "Kitty-chan," the cute cat first appeared on girls' purses during the seventies and spread to stationery, stuffed animals, video games, and even a theme park.

Texting: Schoolgirls didn't invent text messages, but they popularized them. In Japan, young women are still the highest percentage of text messengers.

Virtual pets: Schoolgirls bought tens of millions of Tamagotchi handheld digital pets when they launched in 1996.

Hair coloring: A trend that's here to stay, but that wasn't always the case. Kogals in the mid-1990s kick-started the trend, making fashion statements with their brown, blonde, and even gray locks.

Color contacts: Schoolgirls in the mid-1990s started wearing blue contact lenses, kicking off a *kara-kon* (color contact) boom. By 2005, contact lenses that made the iris look bigger were popular with schoolgirls, because they made their eyes appear larger.

Camera phones: With schoolgirls dragging around disposable and polaroid-style cameras in the 1990s, electronics makers decided to put digital cameras in mobile phones.

Gyaru-go (gal speak): Japanese slang such as "KY" (*kuuki yomenai* or "clueless") started among schoolgirls.

Loose socks: Originally meant for hiking, they made girls legs look skinny and became part of the kogals' essential wardrobe in the mid-1990s. Often still seen on the streets of Shibuya.

Sticker pics: *Purikura* have long been a schoolgirl favorite.

Sticker pictures from Furyu

Chapter 5
KOGALS,
MAGAZINES
& BOOKS

Cover girls

Yonehara Yasumasa is sitting at his desk in his Harajuku office. His graying hair is cut close, and he's decked out in hip-hop gear. Middle-aged or not, it suits him. "I've never liked the obligatory Japanese rules that say you need to dress like an adult—whatever that means," he says. The room is packed with knick-knacks, broken American toys, and boxes and boxes full of photos of women. It's these sexy snaps for which Yonehara is most famous. Taken using Fuji Film's Polaroid-like instant *Cheki* camera, this lo-fi eroticism is his work, and has appeared at exhibitions all over the world.

>>

Yonehara—or Yone as he prefers to be called—was not always a photographer. He was once an editor at *egg* magazine, the most influential girls' magazine of the 1990s, and the *kogal* bible.

Yonehara pushes a photobook forward. "See this," he says pointing to a picture of a stoic, pale girl wearing a neat sailor suit, with her black hair in braids. Her gaze is empty, innocent. "This was the stereotypical image of a schoolgirl in the eighties and nineties. This was what salarymen at the time thought schoolgirls should be." The stereotype was a pure, young girl that could be dirtied up. "Japan was a male-dominated society. Men controlled everything, and girls were supposed to appeal to their desires—until the kogals hit."

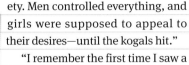

Egg magazine's free pilot issue from 1995

"I remember the first time I saw a kogal," says Yonehara. "I thought she was so cool—she was clearly not someone I could have imagined." *Ko* was short for *koukou* (high school), and *gyaru* was gal—and according to Yonehara these weren't normal girls, they were gals. When the kogals first appeared in the 1990s, he explains, they didn't give a hoot what men thought. "These girls changed society," says Yonehara, "it was a revolution." He whips out a copy of the first issue of *egg*, dated September 1995. The tagline reads "Hyper Idol Station," and the magazine was initially a pin-up rag for men, like a Japanese version of Western guys' glossy *Maxim*. Yone flips past the photos of girls in somewhat dated swimsuits, looking for the section on schoolgirls he used to edit. Inside are photos of tanned kogals wearing frosted make-up, school uniforms with ultra-short skirts, and those ubiquitous loose socks.

Looking like they'd just washed up on a beach—with their streaked hair and tanned skin—the kogals were unlike anything Japan had ever seen. The look wasn't created by girls trying to look Western, it was young Japanese girls challenging the traditional ideals of feminine beauty that had, for so long, dictated pale skin and thick, black hair. Just as Western teens might dye their hair green to make a statement, kogals were taking a stand with their lightened locks. In the early nineties dying one's hair lighter wasn't widely accepted in Japan. Kogals were not merely pushing the envelope but tearing it up into tiny pieces and setting it ablaze.

According to Yone, the first kogals were rich, private schoolgirls rebelling against conformity. "They weren't the type of schoolgirl men could come up with," he says. "It was the result of girls getting together and coming up with a new style they thought was cool." Yone was the first person in the mainstream media to catch on. While the other pages of *egg* were covered with curvy models posing for decidedly male fantasies, his section was filled with realistic, fly-on-the-wall images of high school girls in the street or at home. These girls were stylish, cool, and

Yonehara's kogal pages in *egg* issue 1

Notice the loose socks and dry sock glue on her leg!

チョオリアリズム宣言VOL.1
私たち、自分の気持ちに嘘ついたことないもん

incredibly photogenic. "They didn't need stylists," he says. "They were their own stylist." This was girls' fashion for girls by girls, entirely from the ground up. This look was for them. The photos in *egg*, like the Cheki stacked all over Yone's office, look amateurish, raw, and real. For Yone, that was the point—the sole, true, and honest point. He wanted to capture these girls and show how they existed in the wild.

Despite being in a men's magazine, Yone's pages in *egg* became so popular among the girls appearing in them that ultimately the magazine made the switch to a periodical for girls in late 1996. Circulation spiked and issues like March 1997's "high school girl photographer" special followed, featuring page upon page of Polaroids and snapshots

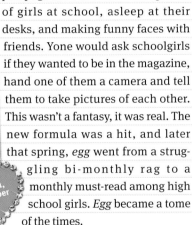

Egg Vol.1, September 1995

of girls at school, asleep at their desks, and making funny faces with friends. Yone would ask schoolgirls if they wanted to be in the magazine, hand one of them a camera and tell them to take pictures of each other. This wasn't a fantasy, it was real. The new formula was a hit, and later that spring, *egg* went from a struggling bi-monthly rag to a monthly must-read among high school girls. *Egg* became a tome of the times.

Much of *egg*'s appeal was the rampant reader participation. In an age before the internet, *egg* offered internet-esque interaction: the reader generated content was what made it so special. Schoolgirls could send along opinionated essays, sticker pictures, or Polaroids covered in colorful graffiti. The pages of the magazine became so personalized by the kogal readers that it became a forum in glossy print that girls could roll up and shove in their school bag.

Yone pounded the pavement, searching the streets in and around Shibuya for the coolest girls and the latest trends. He'd talk to shop clerks, guys passing out flyers, and kids hanging out, to find out which parties the cute girls were going to. And then he'd go to those parties. "I really had to study the street—and then keep studying it," he says. As soon as one trend would start, everyone would copy it, and the trend would become tired. "Then I'd have to find a new trend."

Kogals were not only defining a new type of fashion, but were changing the way magazines covered fashion. "Before kogals, Japanese fashion was mostly top down," says Yone. "People were told what was popular each season, this design or this color. But with kogals, it was about what kids were wearing on the streets. That's how we knew what was popular."

Egg Vol.13, July 1997

Egg magazine became known for the snapshots that showed girls' fashion in the real world. The "street snap" style (as it's called in Japan) spread to other magazines, both men's and women's. "*Egg*," says Yone, "is one of the reasons why street snaps are so prevalent in Japanese magazines today."

One of the girls spotted on the streets was Mami Nakamura, then a fifteen-year-old high school girl and now heading up the Shibuya clothing line BE RADIANCE. "I was just taking a stroll in Harajuku, when I was asked to appear in *egg*," recalls Nakamura. It was 1997. "Girls in the nineties were flashier than previous generations," she says. "Everyone thought they could be models." Nakamura appeared in a few *egg* street snaps and was able to parlay that into regular modeling gigs and

Mami Nakamura in *egg* magazine, 1997

magazine covers of both *egg* and *Popteen*, a charisma clerk job at Shibuya 109, and even TV appearances. "I knew that being on the cutting edge of fashion was more than simply appearing on a magazine cover," says Nakamura. "It meant that if I wore something, the trend would spread." Presumptuous, but true. Like many celebrities, Nakamura was getting free clothes and cosmetics from companies hoping to spike sales and start a new trend. "Japanese people find comfort in being the same," says Nakamura, "but I think there was a strong desire among us to be different, with our own way of thinking."

Ironically, in the desire to be different, a handful of Alpha girls, like Nakamura, created styles that were copied by an army of young women who aspired to be just like them. As a result *egg* began picking the same girls to appear in issue after issue. "At that time," explains Nakamura, "fashion magazines like *egg* were actually less about fashion than the personality of the models. Since the magazines focused on the minutia of the models' daily life, schoolgirls felt closer to them than celebrities on TV." It was easy for schoolgirls to relate to articles on the contents of a model's purse, or how she decorated her room, or an interview with her boyfriend about her character.

But success had its drawbacks, as it led to escalation. "*Egg* began telling girls to put on shorter skirts or tan themselves darker," says Yone. "I didn't like that. *Real* kogals wouldn't listen to editors—real kogals created their own styles." According to Yone, many of the new girls just wanted to be in print—so if *egg* told them to hike up their skirts they'd do it.

Yone remained dogmatic in his approach, wanting girls to appear in the magazine only once. "I didn't want them to become 'models,'" he says, "I wanted them to be someone you'd see on the street. Someone who was real." The editors at *egg*, however, wanted to focus on the popular girls, instead of continually looking for the next thing. What had started out as a revolution in the streets was becoming mainstream.

By this time, the mass media had latched onto the kogal trend. Roaming TV crews in Shibuya became a common sight. The issue of *enjo kosai* (compensated dating) had begun to capture the attention of the press and when they wanted to show schoolgirls on TV, they would show kogals—the "innocent girl" look was out. "I knew the number of actual kogals wasn't as high as TV made it seem," says Yone. "But imagine what people living out in the suburbs or the countryside thought? They thought that's what all the schoolgirls in Tokyo were like."

The look became stock standard for many of the teen girls from the suburbs hanging out in Shibuya. And enjo kosai, which originally meant paying schoolgirls for their company, turned into something more. "There were even girls who were drawn to enjo kosai," says Yone, "because they heard that's what Tokyo girls did." It didn't matter if sex was not

Reader-generated pages of egg

Egg Vol.12,
June 1997

originally involved with enjo kosai; the mass media basically decided it was teen prostitution and blew the trend out of proportion. The latecomers to the kogal scene heard about paid companionship, thought it was a great way to raise cash for brand-name goods, and wanted to give it a try. In turn businessmen started showing up in Shibuya en masse. Yone was appalled. "I told my editor that we shouldn't be using these kinds of girls—that their purpose was totally different. But my editor disagreed and we had a huge row. In the end, *egg* was using only those kinds of girls. So I quit."

🌀 🌀 🌀

As the standard kogal look became mainstream, gal fashion began to get more extreme. The kogal, who were initially rich kids standing up to bourgeois traditions, were replaced with a gonzo breed of working class girls called *ganguro* (literally "black face"). "Fashion got more outrageous," says Yonehara. "But not because it really stood for anything. It was outrageous because that was how girls could get media attention or have their pictures in magazines. Japanese love exaggeration." *Egg* was leading the charge and their girls' fashion became more and more extreme. Models like "Buriteri"—nicknamed after yellowtail-fish teriyaki—graced the magazine's cover with her "Buriteri Style": bleach blonde hair, dark brown skin, frosted lipstick, and eye shadow. Hardly typical, but definitely something people noticed.

"A lot of that extreme fashion was a carry over from *sukeban* culture," says Yone, "where you try to one-up each other." If one girl got a tan, her buddy would get a darker tan. Buriteri, for example, told the tabloid weekly *Shukan Bunshan* that she used make-up foundation imported from Africa to get her dark look. But this obsession with dark skin had very little to do with black culture or Africa—these were girls simply trying to outdo each other. The idea was not to attract guys either, as these girls were largely scorned by society. "I think a lot of girls who get into extreme fashion are just lonely," says Nakamura, "and they're looking for attention." And attention is what these girls got with the media swooping in to see what outrageous fashion trends they were concocting.

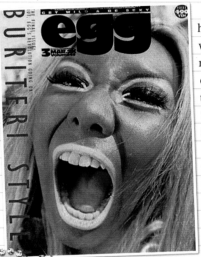

Buriteri on the cover of *egg* March 2000

Much like punk or grunge, what had started out as an act of rebellion was sucked up by the mass media machine. The following generation of schoolgirls wanted to live the fantasy they saw in the glossies, but they just didn't have that edge. "In the nineties, girls were cocky," says Nakamura. "We were models, but we didn't care if we were in magazines or not. We were lax about scheduling, we used nasty language, and weren't exactly professional. But, today's models desperately want to be in magazines and to make a good impression with magazine editors."

By 2000 the pages in *egg* and other magazines dedicated to pictures and letters submitted by schoolgirls had shrunk, and the fashion spreads fattened up. For a few years the amateur snapshots—covered with magic marker doodles of flowers, rosy cheeks, and big globby tears—had given girls a place to express themselves and achieve schoolyard immortality. But the reader-generated pages all but disappeared when *egg* changed publishers in mid-2000, and were replaced with more fashion orientated layouts of gals. Former kogals

MILLION PUBLISHING

Girls on the Street
on magazines

I like egg and *men's egg* because I like their sense of style.

I look at magazines **more often than the internet.**

I think **trends are born** on the street and in magazines.

I'd say my fashion is influenced by the magazines I read.

Yuri Ishikawa

ANDREW LEE

traded in their tans and bleached hairdos for pale skin, parasols, and darker hair. The revolution was over before most girls even realized they were part of something that shook society. "I don't think any of us was aware of a 'movement,'" says Nakamura. "But hearing that people thought we were makes me happy." That lack of awareness is probably why the change in gals' culture has been so permanent. Because for girls at the time it just felt natural.

Egg Vol.158, December 2009

"In the nineties some people were really worried about the changes these girls were making to Japanese society," says Yonehara as he flips through the pages of *egg*. But the changes the loose-sock revolution set in motion were not necessarily a bad thing. The kogals that roamed the Shibuya streets in the nineties were the beginning of the gal culture that has become so dominant in Japan. Compared to earlier generations of women—who were expected to be demure, obedient, and to become good wives and wise mothers—young Japanese woman today are much more confident, brash, and aware of the opportunities life can hold. And they have the kogal to thank for that.

In spring 2012, a new publication, *JK egg*, hit the newsstands. "JK" stands for *joshi kosei* (high school girl) and the mag has all the fashion minutiae a schoolgirl could desire, whether that's "uniform girls' talk," features on the latest *nanchatte seifuku* ("just kidding,"—in other words fake uniforms), or make-up tips for after school. With seemingly endless snapshots of uniformed schoolgirls, *JK egg* harks back to *egg*'s mid-1990's debut. ☺

村上龍

トパーズⅡ

ラ
ブ
&
ポ
ッ
プ

一九九七冬

Novel students

IT WASN'T ONLY the news media who became fascinated with kogals and gal culture. In 1996 novelist Ryu Murakami covered *enjo kosai* (paid dating) in his novel *Topaz II: Love & Pop*, which follows a schoolgirl who prostitutes herself so she can buy a topaz ring. To research the book, Murakami visited *terekura* (telephone clubs), where customers call girls for "dates" and implied prostitution. In 1998 the book was adapted into a feature film.

One of the giants of Japanese literature, Murakami won the prestigious Akutagawa Prize for his 1979 novel *Almost Transparent Blue*, which he wrote as a college student. Fellow Akutagawa Prize winner Risa Wataya won the award (in 2003) when she was a nineteen-year-old college student for her second book, *A Back I Want To Kick*. While still in high school, the then seventeen-year-old Wataya won the prestigious Bungei Prize for her debut novel *Install*. The wunderkind's first two books feature strong high school girl protagonists and sharp prose.

Love & Pop by Ryu Murakami

綿矢りさ

インストール

Install by Risa Wataya

蹴
り
た
い
背
中

綿矢りさ

A Back I Want To Kick by Risa Wataya

125

Phone books

IN 2000, an enigmatic author, who only goes by the name "Yoshi," began passing flyers out to schoolgirls which advertised a *keitai shosetsu* (mobile phone novel) called *Deep Love*.

The novel was written to be read on the tiny screens of mobile phones, and as such the sentences were short, punchy, and lively. The story tells of Ayu, a young Shibuya schoolgirl who sells her body so that a sick kid can get an operation. In the process she contracts HIV. Readers became hooked.

The story was uploaded chapter by chapter as Yoshi was writing it and readers began to email him feedback in real time, which he would then react to. The formula was fresh, new, and popular: Yoshi's cell phone site was getting tens of millions of page views a month, and the first paper version of the book (in what would become a series of *Deep Love* books) was released in late 2002. It was a best seller, selling nearly three million copies and spawning a TV drama, a feature film directed by Yoshi, and even manga for teenage girls.

In an interview in 2004 Yoshi explained why he thought a pot-boiler about a schoolgirl prostitute who gets HIV could become so successful. "Ayu's character is a mirror of contemporary Japanese people," he said. "These girls who sell their bodies are no different from grown-ups who sell their hearts." According to Yoshi, the reason so many young girls became involved in *enjo kosai* (compensated dating) is that, like their parents and other adults, all they care about is the almighty yen.

The mobile phone novel format has been a huge hit with

映画 × 連続ドラマ

赤い糸
オフィシャルブック

The Red String

Special Cover ver.II

young Japanese women and continued to gain momentum in the years following *Deep Love*. Other best-sellers included the high school romance *Akai Ito* (*The Red String*) which sold nearly two million copies as a book and was adapted into a motion picture and TV series. The keitai novel became so successful that it even challenged traditional literature with half of 2007's top-ten best-selling novels (in book form) originating on the mobile phone.

Birds and the bees

GIRLS' MAGAZINES in Japan don't just keep young women abreast of the latest trends and fads, they also supplement an education in something that is insufficiently covered at most schools and typically not discussed with parents: sex ed.

For schools, the difficulty of dealing with politicians (who want traditional family values upheld) and parents (who don't want their kids exposed to explicit or embarrassing subjects) makes instruction difficult. Some teachers would prefer to avoid these headaches and focus on preparing students for college entrance exams. According to *The Asahi Shimbun*, in 2004 the Tokyo Board of Education created a sex ed handbook officially allowing teachers to mention condoms, but prohibited them from telling students how to actually use them.

Popteen brand condoms

That is where girls' magazines come in. They have the power to touch on issues schools can't or won't touch. The magazines don't just offer tips on how to satisfy your boyfriend either. Former porn star turned mainstream celeb Ai Iijima (who died in 2008) penned a serious advice column for *Popteen* called "Love & Sex ER," in which she regularly explained things such as how to use condoms correctly and discussed issues like teen pregnancy and STDs—all of which are supremely important to know about, and all of which are largely left out of the Japanese education system.

More mags for gals

THE RISE OF GAL CULTURE lead to other publications jumping on *egg*'s loose-sock–wearing, tanned schoolgirl band wagon. *Popteen*, for example, has been around as a teen fashion magazine since 1980 but the late nineties saw it begin to focus on gals' fashion. The switch worked, and the magazine regularly sells out on newsstands. "Gal culture has become really mainstream in Japan in the last decade," says *Popteen* editor Wataru Ishihara. The basic concept of the magazine has always been to bring its teen readers the latest fashion trends, plus interviews with celebrities like singers Namie Amuro or Ayumi Hamasaki. It tends to cater to more fashion conscious gals than *egg*, and models even "graduate" from one magazine in order to move to the other. Other magazines have emerged to target smaller segments of the gal phenomenon; such as *Cawaii!*, claiming to be for "gal-type high school girls"; *Ranzuki* for slightly *erokawaii* (erotic cute) schoolgirls; and *Nuts* which is for college-aged "sexy gals."

Schoolgirls on the covers of *Popteen* and *Ranzuki*

Gal talk

THE JAPANESE LANGUAGE is divided into three writing systems: complicated Chinese *kanji* characters, and two phonetic alphabets—*hiragana* for words with no kanji or in place of kanji, and *katakana* for borrowed foreign words and for emphasis (similar to italics).

There has been a long tradition of women contributing to the evolution of the language. In the Heian period (794–1185 A.D.) wealthy girls were educated but it was believed they should avoid the harsh lines of macho kanji characters, and instead taught to read and write hiragana with its delicate feminine curves. Because of this, hiragana was called *onnade* (woman's hand). It was during the Heian era that *The Tale of Genji*, considered to be the world's first novel, was written by Lady Murasaki Shikibu. Today hiragana is used by everyone and is no longer simply considered to be feminine.

Women continue to push both the written and spoken forms of the Japanese language. In the late 1970s and early 1980s, as everything turned cute and pink, so did girls' handwriting—with letters becoming more rounded and adorned with love hearts and other *kawaii* symbols. Then in the nineties schoolgirls began creating *gyaru moji* (gal letters), including Roman, Greek, and even Cyrillic letters in place of standard Japanese characters on their mobile phones. This was especially used for thumbing out emails—creating the ubiquitous emoticons called *kao moji* (face letters), such as (^o^).

Girls in the nineties also began to use a new style of slang based on the way words sound regardless of whether they make sense when written. *Gyaru-go* (gals' language) is fluid, with words going in and out of fashion, but some words enter the general lexicon and never leave.

Gyaru-go slang mixes shortened words, acronyms (using the Roman alphabet), parts of words translated into English, and is heavy

A guide to the language of Shibuya girls

on the use of Japanese prefixes such as *cho* (ultra), and suffixes like *ra* (~er). The language was code lingo parents and teachers couldn't understand. There are even dictionaries available for struggling adults!

Here's a look at some gyaru-go from recent years.

Amura: girls who imitate pop star Namie Amuro.

Buya: Shibuya.

Cho: super, ultra, really. *The* prefix of the mid-to-late 1990s. Most often heard in the expressions *cho beri gu* and *cho beri baddo* ("very very good" and "very very bad").

Deniru: short for *Denizu ni suru*; to eat at Denny's.

***egg* po-zu:** *egg* pose. Posing for pictures with one's hands and arms outstretched, just like the models in *egg* magazine.

GHQ: Going home quickly

Howaito kikku: white kick. Refers to when a joke falls flat. It is a word play on the Japanese words for white (*shiro*) and kick (*keru*), which when put together make *shirakeru* (dampen, fade, spoiled).

JK: *Joshi Kosei* (high school girl)

Konhai: short for *kon no hai sokkusu*; navy blue high socks.

Makuru: short for *Makku ni suru*; to eat at McDonalds.

Manaru: short for *mana mo-do ni suru*; to put your mobile phone on "manner mode."

Maru kyu: 09; short for "Shibuya 109" (*Shibuya ichi-maru-kyu*).

MM: acronym for *maji mukatsuku*; meaning "really pissed off."

No puro: no problem.

OD: *onara deru*; to fart.

Okeru: *karaoke ni iku*; to go to karaoke.

Puriko: *purikura koukan*; trading sticker pictures.

Ru-zu: loose; here referring to loose socks.

Chapter 6
ART

Artists' muse

Class is out for the summer, but schoolgirl Akane Koide is working. The seventeen-year-old artist is painting in an immaculate white studio at the Kaikai Kiki compound in Chiba near Tokyo, getting ready for her first solo exhibition. The cluster of buildings used to be a factory and Koide's studio (which she shares with the artist "Mr."), was converted from the factory office. Her paintings—images of giant penetrating eyes and pursed lipped schoolgirls—are stacked in neat piles on the floor. Splotches of paint dot her black jump suit. "I'm actually the messiest artist in Kaikai Kiki," she says. She is also the youngest member of this art production company created by the world renowned artist Takashi Murakami, and its rising star.

>>

Koide is the daughter of art school grads, so painting and drawing were fostered from early on. As she puts it, her entire home has always smelled of acrylic paint. It was her artist mother who encouraged Koide to enter the Murakami-sponsored GEISAI art fair in 2006, where the canvas paintings of the then fourteen-year-old artist impressed the

most famous Japanese artist in the world. "I was so young," she says, fidgeting with her glasses. "But now that I think about it, I'm still young." A meeting was arranged to which Koide went alone—receiving a stern warning from Murakami, who told her she shouldn't meet men she didn't know without her parents.

"I was a worthless kid back then," says Koide, "I wonder what would have happened to me if I hadn't joined Kaikai Kiki." Murakami runs the collection of artists like a corporation, not at all like an art commune. "I think maybe I was a bit spoiled going in," she recalls. "I knew what the word 'work' meant, but I didn't know what it meant to work. Or what things like deadlines were or how important they were to uphold." Now she has color-coded prints taped to her studio wall, telling when her paintings are expected to be completed. "Even now, I'm not so good with deadlines, but I've gotten a lot better than I was. At first I was thinking about everything like a junior high school girl," she says. "But suddenly, I was expected to not only act like an adult but to think like one too."

Her first year was the hardest. The same month she finished junior high in 2007, she did a live booth painting at the Tokyo Girls Collection.

Soldier girls

JUNIOR HIGH SCHOOLGIRLS. With guns. Shooting each other. *Nobody Dies,* a thirty-five minute short film from the artist known simply as "Mr.", follows a group of schoolgirls who take on their rivals in a capture-the-flag war game with airsoft guns. In most war movies, somebody dies. Here, nobody does. War is *kawaii*. The guns and the girls' camouflaged fatigues are neon cute. The 2008 film is based on Mr.'s painting *It hurts when it hits the bare skin* (2007) that depicts Lolitaesque anime girls in similar outfits. Fourteen-year-old schoolgirls running around the woods shooting each other may seem incongruous, yet somehow fourteen-year-olds doing that dressed in pastel colors isn't. It feels cartoony, yet it's live action. The schoolgirls' outfits look like they're straight out of some anime and each of the girls is a stock-standard anime type; the tough girl, the brain, the cute one, etc.

Nobody Dies is suffocatingly cute, and that's the point. By having the camera leer at these young girls in often uncomfortable close-ups—in the swimming pool or sucking on ice cream—Mr. is unashamed about his *lolicon* (Lolita complex). However, he takes it further than fetishizing these schoolgirls for his own pleasure by exposing the viewer to the *otaku* (geek) subculture that revolves around young idols. "The one thing adults don't have is youth," Mr. says. "Schoolgirls and men live in different worlds, but men are under the delusion that somehow they can enter the schoolgirl world."

Mr.
Nodody Dies,
2008

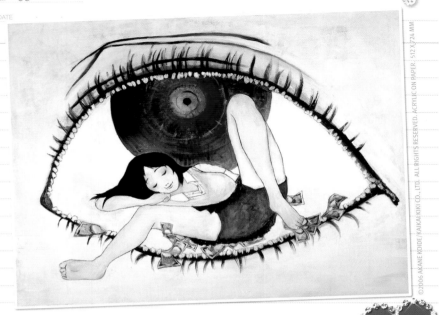

Kaikai Kiki picked TGC because it wanted an event which was packed with Koide's contemporaries—young girls. "I didn't finish my painting, but it was one of the first times people watched me paint," she says. "At first, nobody was watching me and it was embarrassing, but by the end, a crowd had gathered."

Koide has taken what could have been a disadvantage, her age, and turned it into a plus. Her paintings are not nostalgic looks back on the high school experience or commentaries on Japanese youth—they are real time expressions of them.

The ideas for her paintings come to Koide in class, while she doodles in the margins of her notebooks, and sometimes it's the notes that are squeezed in the margins as her sketches fill the page. Koide dreamed of becoming a manga artist and continues to draw upon manga for inspiration as she depicts issues that confront Japanese schoolgirls—issues like *enjo kosai*, which she explored in her work *Show Girl* (2006). The painting shows a schoolgirl lying asleep inside a giant eye. She is

Akane Koide.
Show Girl,
2006

Akane Koide.
When I flipped over I could see the universe, 2007

smiling and her head rests on her arm. Her legs are spread open and we can see up her skirt, but she is wearing shorts under her uniform. Money is scattered about her and she seems to be rolling in cash. She is on show, and the eye in which she rests has rows of teeth ready to consume her.

In 2007, Koide's mentor Murakami wrote that "Koide goes beyond the normal level of a high school student in considering the problems surrounding her. She depicts problems in what appears to be a *shojo manga* (girls' comics) style, while looking for ways to express pain and sympathy." The contrast between the cute, girly style in which she draws and the depth of her subject matter is what makes Koide's work so interesting, especially as her life at school plays such a large part in the choice of her subjects.

In another painting, *When I Flipped Over I Could See The Universe* (2007), a schoolgirl, naked except for the skirt and collar of her sailor suit, floats on her back in mid-air. An apple tree and flowers sprout from her mind while a Cheshire cat-like smiling face grins at her. A hand emerges from a cloud of smoke nearby to drop a test tube into what looks like a giant ashtray on fire. The painting depicts a girl coming to grips with the horrors of nuclear war, and was inspired by a junior high school report Koide had to do on Little Boy, the bomb dropped on Hiroshima.

But like all women, Koide's days as a schoolgirl are numbered; eventually school reports will give way to more adult concerns. Her work shows not only an artist maturing, but a girl becoming a woman, growing not just artistically, but intellectually. She's thinking about going to art college but has been told by her mentor Murakami that art school is boring and a waste of time. "My work is already selling, but there are still things I need to study and need to learn. I'd like to experience it for myself."

🐾 🐾 🐾

Makoto Aida is another artist whose work often depicts schoolgirls, yet contrasts sharply with Koide's work—it comes from an adult male point of view. Aida was one of Japan's enfants terribles, along with Murakami and Yoshitomo Nara, that took the international art scene by storm in the 1990s. These artists had grown up after the war, while the process of rebuilding Japan was in full swing. They experienced the rapid ascent of the Japanese economy during the heady 1980s, and came of age

Makoto Aida.
Azemichi (a path between rice fields)
1991

surrounded by pop-culture. They drew inspiration from this—using the language of manga and anime to convey their message.

Aida is iconoclastic and uncompromising, his work varied and provocative. His themes include sexuality, war, and national identity. And he strives to make the viewer uncomfortable: whether it be videoing himself masturbating in front of a large banner that reads "beautiful little girl," dressing up as Osama Bin Laden for a Saturday Night Live-esque video project, or painting the firebombing of New York by Japanese airplanes.

Makoto Aida.
Picture of Waterfall
(work in progress)
2007~

Girls, however, are a reoccurring motif. "At the age of fourteen, I became obsessed with the magical quality young girls have," he says. "As I get older, the age difference gets wider, and yet the almost magnetic attraction to these girls gets stronger and stronger." But, the artist emphasizes, it's not a romantic interest. Rather, it is a reminder of his youth and his aging. "A major reason why it's not romantic is how desperately impossible it is," he says.

During the late nineties, as gal culture was running rampant, Aida became intrigued. "I think those kogals in the 1990s were originals," he says. "Historically and even globally, they were unique, and I sought a way to portray them." Inspiration came from a group of high school girls squatting on the ground, in Shibuya. "The scene reminded me of besieged warriors who have decided to commit mass suicide." Out of

this, Aida created *Harakiri School Girls*, originally as a poster to advertise his first solo exhibit in 1999, and later as a painting for the Singapore Biennale 2006.

Laced with dark humor, the work shows a group of uniform-clad schoolgirls plunging samurai swords into their stomachs, disemboweling themselves, and slicing off their own heads. The flash of a blade creates a rainbow in the blood spurting from a girl's neck. A stream of blood flows past a curious kitten, karaoke flyers, and discarded tissues, into a drain. The work is gruesomely cute. "*Harakiri School Girls* is an allegory for the distorted mentality of Japanese youth at the time and the atmosphere of Japanese society," Aida explains. "After the Bubble Economy collapsed, I felt that an air of pessimism was spreading through Japan like a virus." Everything might have looked cute and happy, but underneath that veneer seethed dejection and darkness. During the nineties, the number of suicides increased year by year, and according to Aida, Japanese patriotism withered away. These schoolgirls, in their loose socks and school uniforms, symbolize the entire country, killing itself.

Facing page: Makoto Aida. *Harakiri School Girls* 1999~

In *Harakiri School Girls* Aida did not want to simply fetishize uniform-wearing girls or create a modern version of traditional *bijinga* (pictures of beautiful women). Instead he created an homage to the brutal works of ukiyo-e artist Yoshitoshi (1839–1892) and painter Ekin (1812–1876), both known for their ghastly and grotesque work showing decapitations, stabbings, and dramatic scenes of death. "In order to escape the eroticism of the nude, or more explicitly the genitals," says Aida, "I depicted blood and internal organs." And girls in school uniforms. Killing themselves. Smiling.

Aida, who has also included schoolgirls in his paintings *Azemichi* and *Picture of Waterfall*, believes the uniform fundamentally suits the Japanese. Not because they provide conformity, but because they provide a sense of belonging to a group—something that is extremely important in Japanese society. The concept of being "in" or "out" is so culturally ingrained that when parents want to punish small children, they will threaten to lock them outside the house, thereby making them outside the family group. Uniforms, however, offer a sense of being part of something. Yet, over the past two hundred years Japan has become Westernized by cultures that value individuality. "The foundation for Japanese people isn't Western individualism, and our Asian-style group thinking lingers," says Aida. This creates a paradox, and as the artist says, in Japan today "everything is really warped."

"There isn't a great display of originality in Japan," say Aida. "By copying too much from the West, we've slipped into being importers of ideas. And if you always worry about making a mistake, you'll wither away." However, he continues, Japanese people do show originality in low and pop culture. "In the past, for example, there was *ukiyo-e*, while now there is manga and anime. Traditionally, Japan didn't think about exporting its own original subculture, but kept it inside the country, where it could grow and evolve. Kogals are a perfect example of that phenomenon." Kogals are a Japanese original.

🍪 🍪 🍪

The work of Tomoko Sawada also explores the uncomfortable relationship Japanese have with individuality. In the late 1990s Sawada used subway station photo booths to take passport-style portraits of herself. In each photo her hairdo or expression was different. Ultimately, the four hundred monochrome photos she took made up her work entitled *ID400*. The point was that although these were ID photos, none of them identified Sawada.

A master chameleon, Sawada dresses up as the characters in her photos, donning costumes and even going as far as gaining or losing weight depending on the photo. Her work uses the kind of portraits that are part of Japanese life—such as the photos job hunters submit with their applications; portraits taken for the purpose of marriage matchmaking; and

Tomoko Sawada.
School Days/C,
2004.

high school class pictures. For an artist who shows so much of herself, Sawada reveals little. "Taking pictures of myself fits with the way I want to express myself," she says. "The reason why photo art suits me is that it's easy to control and intuitive for me." In 2000, Sawada's acceptance speech for the Canon New Cosmos of Photography award summed up her approach: "I was bound by an inferiority complex. When I started to take pictures, I loved the image of myself in photos because it was attractive and cute. I could make myself look like a model or an actress. As I looked at my pictures again and again, the gap between my real image and the image of me in a picture widened. In other words, my appearance could be easily changed, but my personality did not change."

Sawada's *School Days* series explores this concept further. At first glance the photographs look like regular class photos, taken at various girls' schools, showing a variety of uniforms—from blazers to blouses to

Tomoko Sawada. *School Days/A*, 2004.

sailor suits. But look closely and you'll see that every girl in the photos is actually the same person: Sawada.

Sawada plays the part of each individual student, but her hairstyle, expression, make-up, pose, and even the way she wears her uniforms, is slightly different—giving the impression that the viewer is looking at a group of girls. "By combining make-up with various facial expressions," says Sawada, "it's possible to create a variety of characters." In the photos she captures the things that Japanese students notice about each other: the little differences. The way students are able to express their individuality in a system of conformity.

"I rent school uniforms that are used in TV shows, combined with clothes I've purchased that look like uniforms," she says. "Putting on a uniform fosters a feeling of solidarity." And while not everyone in Japan likes school regalia, the artist believes that uniforms do give Japanese a sense of security.

Sawada, Koide, and Aida, and many other Japanese artists today, use schoolgirls in their work much the same way French Realists like Millet and Courbet painted peasants—schoolgirls represent the common people, they are the soul of the country and bear the brunt of society, they are the ones who keep it going. And sometimes that stress can take its toll.

Back in her studio, Akane Koide describes the inspiration behind one painting that highlights how much her school life affects her work. *Wrist Slit* (2007) shows a schoolgirl with a bandaged wrist holding an X-acto knife. Her forearm is sliced open, and a stream of blood pours out mixing with the essentials of a teen girl's life—cosmetics, a cell phone, a book. Disembodied eyes and lips float in the blood. An extra eye stares out from the back of the girl's head, while another schoolgirl peers in through the window, giving the painting a paranoid air. "High school girls have a wide spectrum of emotions," say Koide, and self-mutilation is fairly common among high girls unhappy

Akane Koide
Wrist Slit,
2007

with themselves, unhappy with their lives. *Wrist Slit* came about when she noticed that one of her friends had cut her wrist. "When I first noticed it, I didn't realize that I was looking at her wrist, but she saw me, and quickly covered it up," says Koide. "I was thinking, 'What? You're doing that?!' I didn't think she was the type. That's why I painted this."

This is just one of the issues she tackles that older artists may be unaware of, and she looks for those that set her apart: "What do I have? What can I offer? Of course, I'm young, and I'm a schoolgirl. There are things I know that adults don't. I have the perspective of still being a kid." ◎

School photos

PHOTOGRAPHER Motoyuki Kobayashi believes schoolgirls are the antidote for suicide, and he has made a name for himself taking photos of them. "I feel that if society looks at the purity of schoolgirls, it can see the future," says Kobayashi. There's hope. These girls represent the Japan of tomorrow. "The purity of young girls' hearts is a common theme in Japan," he says, "like in the works of animator Hayao Miyazaki." Kobayashi tries to capture that purity and has published five photo books of schoolgirl portraits.

スクールガール 6×7 six by seven

小林 基行

In a nation of 120 million, roughly half of the population either were, are, or will be schoolgirls. By photographing them, Kobayashi is capturing that brief moment in a Japanese woman's life when the possibilities are spread before them: get married, don't get married. Work, don't work. Have kids, don't have kids. In this sense "schoolgirl" doesn't simply mean young girls in sailor suits, it describes half the country, it's a stage in a woman's life, it's the female experience.

"Schoolgirls are a symbol of Japanese culture," says Kobayashi, yet he readily admits the girls in his photos exist in an idealized space. "My photos are like a time machine back to the idealized world of my youth." His blue-hued portraits are clean and unadorned. The models are not tanned and wear little to no make-up.

Motoyuki Kobayashi. A page from *Schoolgirl 6x7*

No.

DATE

Motoyuki
Kobayashi.
A page from
*Schoolgirl
6x7*

Schoolgirl Complex
by Yuki Aoyama

Inferiority complex

YUKI AOYAMA has an inferiority complex. He'll be the first one to tell you. And what makes him feel subordinate? Why, schoolgirls.

"As an artist, I'm drawn to the image of the schoolgirl for many reasons. It's an image that symbolizes uniformity—that everyone is the same. It's a nostalgic image that represents a fleeting, ephemeral existence," says the thirty-four-year-old photographer, who has explored this theme in his wildly successful series of *Schoolgirl Complex* photo books, which were even adapted into a feature film in 2013. "The girls are totally aware of this ephemerality, and give their all to enjoying and making it through those years of being a schoolgirl. That's not only appealing, it's also powerful."

According to Aoyama, the title *Schoolgirl Complex* originally referred to his own schoolgirl complex when a schoolboy himself—something that is hardly unique, he adds."For lots of high school boys," he says, "there's an inferiority complex towards schoolgirls."

During school years, says Aoyama, when hormones are raging, schoolgirls are seen as both sexual and holy by their inexperienced male classmates. "When schoolgirls do the slightest thing," Aoyama says, "it can send the hearts of schoolboys racing." But when schoolboys become men, their experience with women is no longer

fantasy. And that period of youth, when everything is fresh and vivid, becomes just a memory.

Aoyama's work, whether he is photographing schoolgirls or other members of Japanese society, examines stock iconography, but he puts his own stylistic spin on the photos, which are a mishmash of reality and fantasy, of memories of what was and what never was. But what is constant is the force the schoolgirls have. Says Aoyama, "I always feel like I'm no match for their power."

Rin Nadeshico.
*Mount Fuji series
Girls Band*,
2007.

Hokusai's daughter

SCHOOLGIRLS CAUGHT IN SPIDERWEBS. Schoolgirls ensnared by tentacles. Schoolgirls rocking out on guitars. This is the work of twenty-five-year-old artist Rin Nadeshico who mixes traditional *ukiyo-e* style imagery with co-eds in school uniforms.

"I adore drawing sailor suits," says the artist, who as a student wore a sailor suit in junior high and a blazer in high school. Taking military-style navy suits and turning them into school uniforms is something she describes as "very Japanese."

Rin Nadeshico is a nom de plume (or brush, rather). *Rin* means cold or dignified, and *Nadeshico* refers to Yamato Nadeshiko, the embodiment of Japan's ideal woman: virtuous, wise,

Rin Nadeshico.
Spring, 2007.

©RIN NADESHICO, ACRYLIC ON WOOD PANEL AND JAPANESE PAPER. 2334 X 910 MM

Rin Nadeshico.
Spring, 2007.

obedient, and brave. (Symbolically, *Yamato* is the ancient name for Japan, while *Nadeshiko* is a type of pink flower). This perfect women is one who can cope with hardship, raise a family, and be prepared to die for the country—which is why military nationalists seized on the concept for World War II propaganda. Nadeshico's work bares elements of this. "The girls in my work are strong, wise, and brave," she says. "Everything I aspire to be."

The paintings and illustrations are also an homage to her hero—the Edo period artist, Hokusai—whose daughter Nadeshico wishes she could have been. (Katsushika Oi was not only Hokusai's daughter, but also his collaborator during the height of his fame).

Nadeshico's work *Shojo Nami* (Young Girl Wave), references Hokusai's *Menami* (Small Wave)—a copy of his wave is visible behind Nadeshico's sailor-suit–wearing schoolgirl. Octopus tentacles wrap around the girl's thighs, making their way up her skirt. While the octopus has often been used as a sexual metaphor in Japanese art (most famously by Hokusai himself), Nadeshico coyly says she simply wanted to draw an octopus.

"Simply copying Hokusai would have been boring," she says. "So I came up with the idea of including something unexpected, like young girls. The contrast fit." For Nadeshico, the stoic schoolgirls in her art are dolls. "The girls never age, they are forever young," she explains. "I was once a schoolgirl too, but sadly I'm getting older." Her plan is to incorporate all of Hokusai's most famous images in her work, in particular his *Thirty-six views of Mount Fuji*, and update them by adding her idealized schoolgirls.

©RIN NADESHICO, WOOD, CANVAS, ACRYLIC. 1000 X 727MM

Rin Nadeshico.
Shojo Nami,
2008.

Keitai Girl

"IN JAPAN, not having a *keitai* is strange," says twenty-seven-year-old artist Noriko Yamaguchi. "Girls need someone to talk to." *Keitai* is short for *keitai denwa* (portable phone), and Yamaguchi's creation *Keitai Girl* is the embodiment of Japanese girls' relationship with their phone.

Yamaguchi's art consists of photographs of herself dressed in costume or naked in various situations that highlight the sense of touch, or of wanting to be touched. As *Keitai Girl* she wears a painstakingly created body suit covered with thousands of cell phone keypads that almost look like fish or snake scales. The idea for *Keitai Girl* first came to Yamaguchi as a high school student when she made a costume using one of her mother's nurse uniforms. Yamaguchi, who wanted to be a manga artist, even created a back story for her character which had her emerging from a factory that disassembles old phones. She officially debuted *Keitai Girl* in 2003 when she was in art school.

Noriko Yamaguchi. *Keitai Girl no.1* (2004)

Aside from the photos, Yamaguchi also performs as *Keitai Girl* in a trio of female dancers who wear matching outfits and do a style of synchronized group dancing called "Para para." The dance has its roots in Eurobeat music and in the nineties was synonymous with the clubs in Shibuya. "Para para is like traditional Japanese summer dancing," Yamaguchi says, "but hyper."

The dancing and the skintight suit give a sensuality to *Keitai Girl*. Her suit is covered in number keypads just waiting to be dialed, inviting people to push her buttons, to ring her bell. "I wanted to create something people would want to reach out and touch," says Yamaguchi. The *enjo kosai* (paid dating) connections are clear. When schoolgirls sold their companionship during the 1990s, they used communication devices like pagers and phones to arrange dates. Technology was the enabler, and *Keitai Girl* is a metaphor for the way that technology connects girls to the world around them.

Girls on the Street on art

Keitai Girl is cool. She's a fun, satirical look at the life of a modern schoolgirl.

I love photography! **I have a toy camera that** I use.

My favorite artists are **Mika Ninagawa** and **Nobuyoshi Araki.**

I like **Mika Ninagawa** too! And **Yoshitomo Nara!**

Both girls are wearing *nanchatte* uniforms

Akane Koide is amazing! **Her work has so many messages.**

Hinae Yoshida and Risa Itou

ANDREW LEE

Chapter 7
GAMES

Playgirls

A lazy rain falls on the streets of Nipponbashi, Osaka's geek district, and maids passing out maid café flyers take cover under dripping shop awnings. Inside the offices of SOFTPAL Inc., an adult video game company, programmers and artists sit hunched over keyboards and tablets, staring at computer screens. At a desk covered with computer game merchandise and stuffed animals sits Noizi Ito, the designer of some of Japan's most popular schoolgirl characters. Her glittery nails are immaculate and ornate, her hair long and curly. Fashionable jackets are draped over her chair and an enormous Louis Vuitton purse rests on her desk beside a light box where she draws when not working from home.

>>

Since she was a teen, Ito has known that simply playing video games wasn't going to be enough. "When I was a student, fighting games were very popular," she says. "All my girlfriends at school were such good players!" For Ito, however, the appeal wasn't just controlling the characters and making them do cool moves, it was the way they looked— the design of the characters. After buying a how-to book on breaking into the industry, she went for interviews at Osaka-based companies like Capcom. "I made it to the second round there," she says, "but didn't get the job." Instead, she ended up at SOFTPAL working on visual novels for home computers.

Visual novels are interactive illustrated computer games with text-driven stories that players must read, and Ito designs and illustrates the games' characters. Make no mistake, these are games for adults with adult content—but the most popular visual novels focus on story and characterization rather than sexual escapades. As the story progresses, players arrive at "decision points" where they choose the plot's trajectory. "In visual novels the story is of course extremely important," Ito says, "but the first thing players are attracted to is the game's art. That's why I like to illustrate them." Many of these games are set in the emotionally charged world of high school and Ito literally draws from experience.

"All women have been schoolgirls at one point," says Ito. "We all like to reminisce about how young we were or how much fun we had.

Yui Inaba from *Flyable Heart*

©2008–2009 UNISON SHIFT/SOFTPAL INC.

I remember when I was in junior high I thought the girls in high school were so grown up, and that they were so cool." And while her characters designs are based more on what she likes than on herself , she notes, "Being a high school girl is probably the best time in a girl's life."

While it may seem odd that young women like Ito work in the very male-orientated world of adult video games, female designers actually have more freedom, and get more famous, creating original characters for these titles than they would elsewhere in the industry working on characters everyone already knows. When a SOFTPAL game that Ito worked on goes on sale, her name is on the box in big letters.

Many gamers buy SOFTPAL's schoolgirl titles because it was Noizi Ito who did the

Noizi Ito's
self-portrait
character

Flyable Heart character designs by Noizi Ito

game art, and scattered throughout the SOFTPAL office are small plastic toy figures, pillow case covers, posters, and other merchandise featuring Ito's cute feminine characters. File folders near her desk are stuffed with her original art for the PC games *Nanatsuiro Drops*, *Flyable Heart*, and *Peace@Pieces*. And in a plastic display case sits a model car covered with stickers of Haruhi Suzumiya—the inter-

Flyable Heart

nationally loved schoolgirl character she designed. Ask her fans why Ito's characters are so popular and they'll tell you her designs have a delicate feminine touch to them. They're not straight up erotic like the characters created by male designers, they're gentle. Her work has even attracted adoration from celebrities like pop idol Shoko Nakagawa.

❧ ❧ ❧

Schoolgirls have been popping up in computer games since the early eighties, generally in what are known as "*bishoujo* games." Bishoujo means "beautiful girl," and games of this kind are mainly targeted at a male audience and revolve around interactions with attractive girls. When companies like NEC and Fujitsu first released computers that could render 8-bit graphics nobody bought them just to play games. Yet, as with many new technologies, pornography sped things up. The use of PCs for gaming increased when a slew of rock-paper-scissors type striptease games were released for these early computers. Companies such as Enix (which would become Square

Tenshitachi no Gogo

Enix), released titles like *Lolita Syndrome* (1983)— in which big-headed, anime-like schoolgirls could be saved from a buzz saw massacre, or have daggers thrown at them to remove their sailor uniforms. The ensuing nudity was a reward for players.

In 1985, computer game developer Jast released *Tenshitachi no Gogo* (*Angels' Afternoon*) for the NEC PC-8801. Aimed at young men, the game was a forerunner to the dating simulators of today. The goal was to win the affection of the female star of a high school tennis club. Graphics were static and players had to type in commands as they chatted up the cute tennis ace and her friend. This was a step up from rock-paper-scissors, and players had to build a relationship with the character in order to proceed through the game. Although *Tenshitachi no Gogo* was an adult title featuring steamy scenes with high school girls, the game skirted controversy by using anime-style art. It didn't feature "real" girls; in other words, it was merely fantasy.

While titles like *Tenshitachi no Gogo* hinted at what was to come for ensuing generations of X-rated games—including early dating sims like *Gakuen Monogatari* (*Academy Story*, 1987) and *Dokyusei* (*Classmates*, 1992)—not all the games were erotic games (*eroge*). Since home video games consoles were sold in toy stores, they were logically viewed as toys by the game industry, and strictly self-regulated regarding adult content. Companies like Nintendo and SEGA (and later Sony) played Big Brother, only approving games for their consoles that didn't cross the line. Personal computers, on the other hand, did not fall under these regulations because they were (and still are) an open platform, giving computer game developers more freedom in the type of titles they developed.

Developers like Konami created family friendly dating games (*ren'ai* games) for home consoles, including their *Tokimeki Memorial*. These were smut free, and wildly popular. The first game in the *Tokimeki* series sold over half a million copies and spawned countless sequels. The game's plot is gooey sweet: players try to get a girl to confess her love under a tree, which, according to legend, means the couple will live happily ever after. The story, while told from a male point of view, had so much cross-gender appeal that Konami made a version for female players called *Tokimeki Memorial: Girl's Side*, which allowed a schoolgirl character to pursue a cast of male students and added things like the ability to go shopping. Yay, shopping.

Konami later pushed the boundaries of digital dating with its 2009 Nintendo DS game, *Love Plus*. The first half of the game is a get-the-schoolgirl dating simulator, while the second half is open-ended.

In the game, players can email their girl-friend, call her or study with her, and use the Nintendo DS's stylus to affectionately caress their girlfriend's arm or cheek. Since the game is in real time, players even have to remember their girl's birthday, unless they want to upset her. As a public-ity stunt, one gamer even "married" a schoolgirl character from *Love Plus* and took her on a honeymoon to Guam. Other players were simply satisfied to buy real cakes for their in-game sweetie on her birthday.

While dating sims like *Tokimeki Memorial* were about getting girls to go on "dates," visual novels put more emphasis on following a story rather than pursuing a goal. In 1997 PC game developer Leaf popular-ized the visual novel with their title *To Heart*. Much like very early bishoujo games (except infinitely longer), players of visual novels read on-screen text while looking at illustrations and then make decisions that affect the plot line. The point is not to simulate relationships, but to absorb the player in an interactive story through sound and graphics. Think of them as romance novels for computer nerds.

Akari Kamigishi
from *To Heart*
by Leaf

© AQUAPLUS

To Heart told the story of high school student Hiroyuki Fujita as he interacts with a bevy of his female classmates—including maid robot schoolgirls! The game wasn't Leaf's first foray into visual novels, but defined the studio's style, and set the benchmark for other companies. Their fresh and inventive characters have since been recycled by countless other PC game developers into visual novel stereotypes. *To Heart* was such a hit that the number of adult titles almost doubled the year it was released, and more than tripled the year after that. *Kanon*, a 1999 visual novel for adults from game developer KEY, about high schoolers with amnesia, would go on to sell three hundred thousand copies. Both games were later ported to home consoles without the adult content, and the all-ages console versions were even ported back to the PC. Which proves, if anything, that visual novel players don't play the titles just for the adult scenes. No, really! The stories, the characters, and the catchy music were so appealing that the games didn't actually need the erotic content.

Games fair maidens play

OTOME GAMES, literally "maiden games," let teenage girl players pick their ideal beau from a harem of *bishonen* (beautiful young boys). The genre started in 1994 with *Angelique*, a Japan-only dating sim for girls in which young Angelique vies to become Queen of the Universe while chatting up young studs. Since the game was aimed at teenage girls and featured a princess, it was filth-free. Princesses are not meant to be smutty. The game was a hit, spawning sequels, manga, anime, and a new sub-genre.

In-game screen from *Vitamin X Evolution* by HuneX

"The appeal is more than falling in love with dreamy male characters," says HuneX's development director Munehiro Tada. Girls play otome games for the artwork, the story, and the swoon-inducing voice acting. In HuneX's *Vitamin* series of otome games, players take the role of a female teacher assigned to help her school's worst class graduate. They're handsome bad boys, but they're total nitwits. And since it's a *renai* (dating) game, there's a catch: if the player corrects her pretty male students, then those dreamboats will like her less. But if she doesn't correct the underage students, they will like her more, but remain dumb as doorknobs. The game features vaguely academic quizzes on school subjects like geography, math, science, history, and literature. It's like homework, but better looking.

Vitamin X Evolution characters

"What makes our dating sims unique is the complex relationships," says Tada. Besides female teachers getting romantic with young male students, HuneX's otome game plots also include married women getting involved with single young dudes. "Those might seem like risky scenarios, but the games don't destroy the pure image of otome."

© 2008 D3 PUBLISHER © HUNEX

As the number of adult games for PCs increased, more and more of them were ported to home consoles. "In keeping with the strict guidelines for home console titles, any PC games with erotic content were given a drastic full-scale overhaul," says Munehiro Tada, development director at HuneX, a game developer known for porting PC games to home consoles. When edited versions of adult games appeared on home consoles during the late 1980s and early 1990s, players could tell something was missing, because the edited-out erotic elements had been the main content. But as more and more titles emerged that did not simply feature sex and actually had stories you could follow (such as *Kanon* or *Air*), they reached a wider audience.

However, since these kind of games deal with romance and even adult situations among high school students, it is difficult to bring visual novels and their "over-eighteen" content to a Western game-playing audience—especially as the characters in the game are younger than the age required to purchase the games. "I

The *nakige* (crying game) *The Eternity You Desire*

think because of the religious morals in the West," says Tada, "certain themes have a hard time being accepted." Yet in Japan visual novels make up the vast majority of the PC games market and the inevitable anime and manga spin-offs mean these games are inching closer to the mainstream. And while not all feature schoolgirls, they do dominate.

In summer 2010, the game company behind Love Plus, Konami, launched a vacation for players and their digital squeezes. For ¥39,800

(US$405), a bus tour whisked the happy couples away to Atami, the Japanese city that provides the setting for Love Plus, for two days and one night. Gamers and their (virtual) gal pals visited locations that appeared in the game, such as the city's castle and shrines.

At various sites throughout Atami, there were augmented reality set-ups so real gamers could use an iPhone app to snap AR photos with their digital girlfriends for photo memories. And when their day of fun was over, Love Plus players retired to their hotel, digital lady friends in tow. Each tour member, however, was put up in a room for one.

This was far from the only real world Love Plus cash in. Bakeries have sold Love Plus cakes during Christmas, a Tokyo curry restaurant offered a free drink for patrons who bring their virtual girlfriends, and Konami,

The Eternity You Desire

which launched New Love Plus for the Nintendo 3DS in 2012, offered a monthly ¥315 subscription service to get emails from Love Plus as well as an official Love Plus branded credit card. Priceless.

🌀 🌀 🌀

School settings are a logical choice for dating games—for both male and female players, alike. "'Schoolgirls' is a keyword that recalls a nostalgic period all Japanese people share," says Hirohiko Yoshida, CEO of PC

Haruka Suzumiya and Mitsuki Hayase from *The Eternity You Desire*

game company ACID. "That time of junior high and high school is, in particular, a transitional period," Yoshida continues. "There are people who feel they've lost something, who feel that they didn't want to grow up, or didn't think they'd end up like they have," he adds. "The fantasy of returning to the days of their youth makes for an easy place to play."

These games are typically played by adult males, but that doesn't mean they are playing the games *as* adult males. Most guys have their first crush on a girl at high school—when teenage hormones are raging—so it's not really any surprise that bishoujo games set in high school often feature sexual content. But that's not *all* these games are about: it is just one aspect of game play, just as it is one aspect of being a teenager. "In visual novels, as in adventure games, the protagonist is the player," says Yoshida. "The game is played from the first person perspective so it's very immersive." The players effectively become their high school-aged avatar. But the characters are drawn in an anime style and often have blue, purple, and green hair so the fantasy element is pronounced. Even so, the games are quite regressive and the cute illustrated schoolgirls can have a powerful effect on players' emotions. Some players report being moved to tears—and these games have become widely known as *nakige* (crying games).

Nanatsuiro Drops characters designed by Noizi Ito

Nakige are known for their sense of melancholy. Take 2001's *Kimi ga Nozomu Eien* (*The Eternity You Desire*), for example, which was released by eroge label âge, a division of ACID. Soon after high school student Takayuki Narumi falls for his classmate Haruka Suzumiya, she goes into a coma after a car accident. Depressed and shocked, Takayuki develops post-traumatic stress disorder and becomes involved with Haruka's best friend, Mitsuki. "To put it simply, a nakige brings players to tears as they read the in-game text," says Yoshida. "In the past, adult games were seen as pornography in Japan, so were called *nukige*, or games to masturbate to. For players, nakige aren't about sexual climax, but about relieving stress via shedding tears. In other words, nakige put less importance on matters of the flesh and more on matters of the heart."

The emotion most often associated with nakige is *moé*. The kanji used for the word means "to bud," yet it also sounds like the Japanese for "to burn"—creating a word-play that is most often associated with the kind of cute, young schoolgirl characters with giant eyes that some *otaku* find appealing. While it's been described as the warm fuzzy feeling you get in the pit of your stomach, the concept keeps changing along with tastes and trends. According to Noizi Ito, "what one person thinks is moé could be totally different from what another thinks is moé." For her, school uniforms are very moé. "The way they look and the way they are designed is beautiful," she says explaining that their appeal is how "eye-catching" they appear on a group of students. However the uniforms she creates for the characters in games differ from the real deal. "Actual uniforms put more importance on proper discipline and regimen," she says. "My design may have a ribbon like a real uniform," she says, pointing to a uniform design for the game *Nanatsuiro Drops*, "but I make that ribbon larger so that it looks cuter. In reality, school isn't like this—this is a dream," Ito says. "The uniforms I design might be flashy, but I still want them to seem possible in the real world." Even if the game's stories are merely fantasy. ✎

Furyu sticker pictures

Stuck on you!!

IN 1995, a female employee at Tokyo video game developer Atlus came up with *Print Club*: a photo booth that takes small pictures and prints them out on sticky paper. The sticker pictures were originally intended for business cards, but schoolgirls got a hold of them and made them their own. Affectionately known as *purikura*, *Print Club* set Japan ablaze with teens lining up outside arcades for the low-res digital snaps. By the late 1990s, the market exploded and game company after game company released sticker picture machines hoping to catch schoolgirls' fancy.

Compared to the simple, low-tech *Print Club*, today's sticker picture machines run on hi-tech software and are outfitted with powerful, state-of-the-art cameras and studio quality lighting. The sticker picture machine is powered by a computer running cutting edge software that interprets the images taken by the camera. Face recognition software is able to make eyes bigger and faces smaller—both desirable kawaii traits. Other software can do things like lengthen hair, whiten skin and even slim down hips.

During the 1990s, girls collected sticker pictures, traded them, and pasted them in notebooks they carried around called *purikura techo*. Hard copies of the pics are still popular, but the latest sticker picture machines can

send digital copies directly to girls' cell phones so they can swap them via email.

To keep up and set the latest trends, Tokyo-based sticker picture maker Furyu, for example, has groups of schoolgirls test out new machines and takes their feedback into account when designing new machines. Furyu was also one of the first companies to use fashion models from girls' magazines to promote sticker picture machines—now standard practice. "All girls want to be cute," says Furyu representative Reiko Kadosawa, "and sticker picture machines show the cutest side of a girl."

The appeal isn't just the sticker pictures. According to Furyu's Kadosawa, "When girls use sticker picture machines, they're not only paying for the pictures, but also the time together with their friends taking those pictures." Girls come up with poses together, write messages on the pix, and trade photos with their friends. "Sticker pictures are a part of schoolgirl life," she adds. "They've become a communication tool."

Sticker pictures and photo booth from Furyu

Sensei, may I take your order?

TOKYO OTAKU (geek) district Akihabara is home to an endless number of maid cafes, where staff in frilly dresses wait tables and serve grub. JK Cafe isn't your typical maid cafe. It's a schoolgirl cafe.

JK Cafe, or "Joshi Kosei" (high school girl) Cafe, aims to tap Japan's endless fascination with schoolgirls. But JK Cafe isn't staffed with young women pretending to be schoolgirls—the waitresses *are* schoolgirls, bringing anime and manga fantasies to life by allowing adult customers the chance to talk to real-life girls in sailor suits. According to the cafe's management, the restaurant is capitalizing on the schoolgirl's position as Japan's eternal idol.

While other Akihabara establishments that employ schoolgirls have been busted for enjo kosai (paid dating), JK Cafe's management claims this place is different, adding that it's simply a schoolgirl-themed cafe that employs actual schoolgirls. That's it.

JK Cafe hires students as an after-class gig, but school life doesn't end when the girls' part-time job begins. At maid cafes, waitresses address patrons as "master," but here, the gals address them as "sensei" (teacher).

JK Cafe, or "Joshi Kosei" (high school girl) Cafe

"Everyday is a blast," says Tsumugi, a seventeen-year-old JK Cafe waitress. "I get to talk to various sensei and hang out with other girls my age. "JK Cafe feels like real school."

Unlike real school, staff wear anime-inspired sailor suits as they serve rice omelets, curry, and French toast as well as fizzy drinks and booze—including "original schoolgirl cocktails." Oh, and there's no homework.

Girls on the Street on games

The schoolgirls in video games are so *moé*!! And *kawaii*!

Where do I play games? At home.

I like simulation games on the Nintendo handheld.

I go to *purikura* about five times a month! It's a great way to remember fun times!

Rie Murai

ANDREW LEE

Girl fight

AS GAME CHARACTER DESIGNER Noizi Ito points out, "In the real world, schoolgirls are not physically strong. But mixing that helpless image with the fighting power of men makes for a complex character." This is exactly why schoolgirl characters in fighting games tend to be so popular.

Years before iconic game heroines like *Tomb Raider*'s Lara Croft or *Street Fighter II*'s Chun-Li, the schoolgirl Athena Asamiya was one of the pioneering female video game action stars. Athena first appeared internationally in 1987 as a pink-haired schoolgirl blessed with psychic powers in game company SNK's side-scrolling arcade game *Psycho Soldier*—where she defeated baddies in a crumbling urban sprawl while wearing a navy blue school uniform. While *Psycho Soldier* was not a fighting game per se, Athena was to re-emerge in SNK's *King of Fighters* series in 1994. Initially, however, SNK put her in various red smocks on the grounds that the appeal of a sailor outfit might be lost on foreign players. Game fans, however, begged SNK to let Athena whop ass in her sailor suit, and *The King of Fighters '99: Evolution* finally featured her once again in full sailor suit garb. She also appeared in uniform in *The King of Fighters XI* and *The King of Fighters XII*.

But perhaps the most iconic fighting schoolgirl character is Sakura Kasugano from Capcom's *Street Fighter* series. Sakura first appeared in the 1996 arcade version of *Street Fighter Alpha 2*, just as kogals were beginning to make waves in the Japanese press. Sakura, however, was just a sailor-suit–wearing, fresh-faced kid in a skimpy skirt, headband, red sneakers, and matching red sparring gloves. Initial designs had Sakura wearing a kimono, but Capcom decided it wanted to pitch players a curveball by including a character with a twist.

Athena Asamiya from SNK's *King of Fighters* series

"Even I was taken aback when I first saw Sakura," says *Street Fighter IV* producer Yoshinori Ono. "I mean, a schoolgirl? That really threw me." The sailor uniform, symbol of schoolgirl innocence, clashed with the game's rogue's gallery of hard nosed brawlers. They looked like fighters. Sakura did not. "The choice of a sixteen-year-old having fisticuffs was not haphazard, but deliberate," says Ono. "She has a certain purity or innocence about her that is simply not present in the other characters and that makes her stand out ." As a design choice Sakura could not have been better.

Sakura kicking butt!

Initially there was concern that the character might be a flash in the pan when the country's cultural mood shifted, but the fears were unfounded. "She's still around more than a decade later and fans still adore her," says Ono. The character's appeal rests in her vulnerability: she looks like a regular schoolgirl, but those sparring gloves and bandanna give away the ass-kicking that's in store. In 2009, Sakura appeared as an exclusive character in the home console versions of *Street Fighter IV* to entice players to purchase the title.

Sakura Kasugano as she appears in Capcom's *Street Fighter IV*

© CAPCOM USA

Comic Icons

The smell of roasted beans and the sound of Stevie Wonder fills the air of the trendy Kobe café as Miwa Ueda takes a sip of her coffee. It's a far cry from the *manga* cafes up the street, where people shell out to select reading material from stacks of comics, many of them featuring school-girls, in uniform and out. Ueda is well represented in those and other manga cafes all over Japan. She's the artist of the manga *Peach Girl*, a prime example of the ubiquitous combination of school-girls with manga, and by extension, *anime* >>

Miwa Ueda's popular, high-school–themed romantic comedy first appeared in the teen-geared comic magazine *Bessatsu Friend*—whose title is a Japanese pun on "best friend." The "peach girl" of the title is high school girl Momo (Peach), who has a dark complexion and is often mistaken by others for a bimbo kogal. As if this wasn't bad enough, matters are made worse by Momo's only friend, the two-faced Sae, who takes great delight in spreading rumors about her. The comic

Momo—not a bimbo kogal

KODANSHA COMICS

is a *shojo* (young girl) *manga* targeted at a female audience, just as there are also comics targeted at young males dubbed *shonen* (young boy) *manga*. Of course, *shojo manga* and *shonen manga* differ in style, story and themes in order to match the interests of their respective audiences—but schoolgirls are a character type that pop up in both.

While *Bessatsu Friend* is targeted at a teenage market, there is a significant number of readers who are in their twenties and thirties. "A lot of OLs buy *Bessatsu Friend*," says Ueda, using the abbreviation for "office ladies," a reference to female office workers. "I think they probably buy the magazine out of a feeling of nostalgia for their high school days." Ueda's goal was to make something fun for schoolgirl readers, but the manga also drew upon her own experiences. "When I was a schoolgirl, my skin was naturally quite dark," Ueda says. "So maybe Momo is like me in some ways . . . but I don't go around punching other people! Momo may seem as though she's very strong and tough, but actually she's really quite sensitive and weak."

Momo was a character who suited the mood and trends of the late 1990s. "I would probably draw a completely different character today," says Ueda, "but it worked back then." *Peach Girl* was a product

Peach Girl, tough but sensitive!

© 1998 MIWA UEDA / KODANSHA COMICS

of the *kogal* boom, though at that time it was still uncommon for schoolgirls to dye their hair brown, let alone blond like Momo. Ueda recalls how she would get letters from her schoolgirl readers, letting her know that they thought Momo looked like one of the girls out of kogal magazine *egg*.

"I started to feel slightly worried that I was coming in on the tail end of the kogal boom. Though it didn't end up being a problem," Ueda says. "There is a fine line between capturing the moment and quickly becoming passé." Her characters did talk about topics that were very much in the air during the late 1990s, but *Peach Girl* was not written in the schoolgirl slang of the times—a choice that was made, according to Ueda, because she was thinking about readers in the future and she didn't want her manga to smack heavily of the past and become unnecessarily dated.

The cover of *Peach Girl* volume 1, 1998

Ueda succeeded as a manga artist when she was just barely older than her protagonist. While she was still a high school student, she began submitting her manga for publication after her parents told her that manga god Osamu Tezuka had made his professional manga debut at the age of only seventeen. "My personal deadline was to also go pro by the time I was seventeen," Ueda recalls. And she very nearly made it too—her debut work was published just one year late.

There are manga for everybody—schoolgirls, salarymen, teenage dudes, and housewives—and on every subject, ranging from high school romance to the office politics of the business world. Besides the genres of shojo manga and shonen manga, demographics also include—but are by no means limited to—*kodomo muke manga* (manga aimed at kids), *seinen* manga (aimed at young men), *seijin* manga (aimed at adult men), and "Ladies' Comics" (aimed at adult women).

Though manga entered a golden age in Japan during the 1950s and the genre has gone on to achieve acceptance and popularity all over the world, its heritage can be traced to Japan's long and proud history of illustration and decorative arts. As early as the eleventh century, Japanese artists were inking scenes on scrolls that would reveal a tale as they were unrolled. Later, during the Edo period (1600–1868), comic pictures and *fuzokuga* (genre paintings) were influenced by daily life

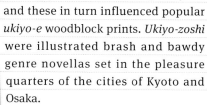

The first schoolgirl manga character: Miss Haneko Tonda

and these in turn influenced popular *ukiyo-e* woodblock prints. *Ukiyo-zoshi* were illustrated brash and bawdy genre novellas set in the pleasure quarters of the cities of Kyoto and Osaka.

The term "*manga*" first appeared in the late Edo period when artists such as Hokusai published picture books of their work, the most famous of these being the *Hokusai manga*. These, however, were simply collections of images, not narrative-driven like manga in the modern sense. By the end of the nineteenth century, American and European multi-panel comic strips had started to make their way to Japan as the country opened itself to Western influences. These foreign imports found instant appeal, and four-panel comics began to appear as a regular feature of Japanese newspapers and magazines.

The father of modern manga is largely considered to be artist Rakuten Kitazawa, who was responsible for founding the magazine *Tokyo Puck*, which was based on the English satirical magazine *Punch*. Kitazawa also created the first schoolgirl manga character with his 1928 comic *Miss Haneko Tonda*, about a young girl who had an obsession with Western fads and fashions.

During the Second World War, the Japanese government banned the import of comic books from the West, but comics flooded back into the country during the American occupation of Japan in the years immediately following the war. During this period, male artists came to dominate the manga industry; it was male artists, not female, that were creating stories targeted at the shojo market, and manga found its greatest creative voice and style when Osamu Tezuka began to debut manga such as *Astro Boy*, *Kimba the White Lion*, and the shojo manga *Princess Knight*.

Tezuka's shojo classic began running in serialized form in 1953 in the girls' magazine *Shojo Club*, and it later became a televised anime. The story follows the adventures of Princess Sapphire. The hook? She has the blue heart of a boy and the pink heart of a girl, and in order to assume her place as heir to the throne, she must pass herself off as a boy or legally lose her right to succession. The blurring of gender lines and gender roles appealed to young girls with its empowering fantasy in which they could experience male roles second hand—a theme that would become a dominant one in the world of shojo manga. The *Princess Knight* storyline also contained magical elements, foreshadowing a genre that would prove popular in future generations.

The mid-fifties saw the advent of the monthly shojo manga *Ribon* (Ribbon) and *Nakayoshi* (Good Friends), and an increasing number of weekly comics aimed at boys, marking a clearly defined schism between the types of manga. More girls' manga meant a bigger market;

手塚治虫 漫画全集

リボンの騎士

© TEZUKA PRODUCTIONS CO., LTD.

Tezuka's Princess Knight

a bigger market meant female artists had a better chance at becoming professional *mangaka* (manga artists); and the ensuing decades saw more female mangaka than ever.

As the shojo audience grew and grew up, the comics shifted from pre-teen to teen and to increasingly mature themes. Instead of male manga artists trying to imagine what girls were thinking or what the shojo audience wanted, female mangaka were able to create comics for girls that expressed the thoughts and feelings of their characters in a more authentic way. The methods that were used to convey those thoughts and feelings were not always the most realistic, but they were without a doubt expressive—such as using baroque floral motifs and decorative costumes for example, in order to symbolize emotions that were in tune with the sentiments of female readers.

"Impressions and feelings are much stronger when we are teenagers, because that is a time in our lives when we experience so many things for the first time," Ueda notes. The schoolgirl comics from shojo manga artists like Riyoko Ikeda, author of popular series *The Rose of Versailles*, vividly expressed in print the romantic and passionate feelings caused by those memorable first loves and agonizing first break-ups. This close relationship between female mangaka and their female readership led to not only pushing the boundaries of art, but the frontiers of sexuality.

By the 1970s, a group of young, female mangaka that included Riyoko Ikeda, Keiko Takemiya, and Ryoko Yamagishi, among others, had emerged. All of these women were born in the post-war era—1949, to be exact—and therefore came to be known as the Year 24 Group, referring to the Japanese calendar year Showa 24. These mangaka confronted issues of sexuality by exploring romance and gender roles through their work, and it was thanks to them that the *shonen ai* or Boys' Love (BL) genre gained widespread acceptance and popularity in the seventies.

After the publication of Keiko Takemiya's manga *In the Sunroom* (1970), which features the first male-to-male kiss in mainstream manga, fellow artists of the same generation began to explore male–male relationships for the enjoyment of their straight female readership, through stories that might for example feature beautiful androgynous boys in boarding schools involved in homosexual relationships. Toward the end of the decade, schoolgirls even got an

The Rose of Versailles by Riyoko Ikeda

entire magazine dedicated to Boys' Love called *June*, in which teens could peruse storylines about love affairs between beautiful boys or the trysts of handsome, rich, gay men, or even tales of yakuza smitten with their fellow gangsters. The characters were typically slender and delicate—womanly, even—and were not to be confused with the hairy muscle-bound beefcakes of "Men's Love" manga, which were created for, and usually by, gay men.

The long running BL manga magazine *June* (2010)

While BL manga sometimes touched on issues of sexual politics such as discrimination against gay couples, this would be merely a plot device to raise the stakes, create tension, and move the male protagonists closer together. BL manga artists seemed less interested in promoting political issues or gay rights, and more focused on the all-important concerns of entertaining and enthralling their female readership. Since the typical BL relationship was a pitcher–catcher dynamic, the manga allowed schoolgirls freedom in their sexual fantasies. They could identify with either character—or both. The absence of females in the manga also had the effect of moving the comics further into the world of fantasy. Young female readers could dream about more than romance without being forced to come face to face with the realities of sex with a male partner. If the idea of boys, as beautiful as they were, was not appealing, the 1970s saw the rise of the *shojo ai* or Girls' Love (GL) genre. Year 24 Group mangaka Ryoko Yamagishi explored the relationship between two schoolgirls attending a French boarding school in her 1971 manga *Shiroi Heya no Futari* (Our White Room). Yamagishi was picking up where early twentieth-century author Nobuko Yoshiya left off—Yoshiya penned novels about pure, romantic friendships between young girls. Yamagishi's works carried feminist themes of young women battling against a male-dominated society and were labeled "Class S" with the "S" representing "shojo," "sister," "sex," or any combination thereof. Her work is a reflection not only of her own sexuality, but also of the rapid growth in the number of girls' schools at the time. Both Girls' Love and Boys' Love manga have gone on to find audiences in the West as *yuri* and *yaoi* manga and anime.

🍃 🍃 🍃

Just as the movies in the mid-seventies had been invaded with films featuring hordes of tough schoolgirls, this decade also brought these hard-as-nails kids to the forefront of manga with Shinji Wada's *Sukeban Deka*, which chronicles the adventures of sailor-suit–wearing, yo-yo–slinging bad girl Saki

Sukeban Deka
by Shinji
Wada

MEDIA FACTORY INC.

なな子SOS
吾妻ひでお
Hideo AZUMA

Nanako SOS
by Hideo
Azuma

HAYAKAWA PUBLISHING

Asamiya. The hero-ine manages to escape from jail only to be forced by the government to take on the role of undercover cop whose mission it is to fight crime in high schools and juvenile prisons. While *Sukeban Deka* was a shojo manga aimed at young girls, it wasn't frilly-dilly story time. This stuff was unflinch-ing, with hard-nosed tales of brutality and blood. *Sukeban Deka* also had no qualms about showing its underage shojo her-oine drinking, smoking, and fighting.

It was no surprise that *Sukeban Deka* found appeal across the gender lines. This is a manga that went on to inspire a generation of male manga artists to create their own version of the tough girl in a sailor suit. The seinen manga *Nanako SOS*, for example, which ran from 1980 to 1986, featured a green-haired, sailor-suit–wearing crime-fighting girl who develops super powers (including the ability to fly!) after an unsuccessful science experiment causes her to lose her memory. The manga was created by Hideo Azuma, considered by many as the father of the *lolicon* (Lolita complex) genre, which features very young girl characters in suggestive or even sexual situations. *Nanako SOS* mixes Lolita-cute with comedy and science fiction.

Interest in schoolgirls blazed through the mass media in the eighties, led by the pop idol group Onyanko Club and chronicled by the publication of *The Illustrated Schoolgirl Uniform Guidebook*. And uniform-wearing schoolgirl characters like *Sukeban Deka's* Saki Asamiya and *Nanako SOS*'s eponymous heroine spearheaded a brand new trend that led to one of the most successful manga franchises in history.

"I thought sailor suits were cool," says manga editor Fumio Osano. "So I wanted to create a manga in which the main character wore one." At the time he was in discussions with mangaka Naoko Takeuchi, who wanted to do a girly equivalent of every young boy's favorite, *Super Sentai Series* (known as *Power Rangers* in the US), replacing the male characters with a squad of *mahoshojo* (magical girls). This was the magical-girl genre that Tezuka had first played with in *Princess Knight*, a genre that had gone on to develop further in the sixties with *Secret Akko-chan*, a manga and anime inspired by the US television show *Bewitched*. Osano felt that *Power Ranger*–style uniforms wouldn't work in this scenario. "We needed something softer," he says. So he suggested putting Takeuchi's team of super heroines in the kind of sailor suit uniforms typically worn by junior high school girls. The result was *Sailor Moon*, which became the biggest shojo hit of the nineties.

The *Sailor Moon* storyline is centered around klutzy schoolgirl Usagi, who is actually a Moon Kingdom princess reincarnated on Earth in the body of a junior high school student. In possession of magical powers, she becomes the leader of a group of color-coordinated, sailor-suit–wearing Sailor *senshi* (warriors), and together they defend the universe from destruction. Osano believes that while the sailor uniform carries with it a nuance of Japan's militaristic past, most people also see it as

Sailor Moon, powerful and eyecatching

representing youth, beauty, and purity—attributes that are a perfect thematic match for *Sailor Moon*. "It has impact," says Osano. "A group of students wearing sailor suits or uniforms is both powerful and eye catching." But also expressed through their clothes is the fleeting nature of their youth. "The sailor uniform can also be seen as a symbol of the cocoon young women exist in before entering womanhood," says Osano.

The manga and the anime versions of *Sailor Moon* were a huge international hit, spawning a live-action television show, stage

KODANSHA COMICS

Naoko Takeuchi's mahoshojo hit *Sailor Moon*

© NAOKO TAKEUCHI

musicals, and an extraordinary variety of goods ranging from dolls to electric piano keyboards. And while *Sailor Moon* was aimed at the under-twelves, the franchise incorporated mature subject matter into the kiddy content. As the series gained popularity, *Sailor Moon* pushed the envelope by featuring one of the first openly lesbian couples in mainstream television cartoons (Princess Neptune and Sailor Uranus). In 2013, promotions began for a twentieth anniversary *Sailor Moon* anime.

So what is it about the mahoshojo genre that makes it draw such a huge global audience? "Girls like these stories because the characters transform—they become cute," says Miwa Ueda. "Anyone can transform, anyone can change the way they look—it's like with cosmetics."

Manga artist Arina Tanemura, best known for *Kamikaze Kaito Jeanne*, pushes that analogy further and sees magic actually acting as a substitute for cosmetics: rather than using lipstick and blush, Tanemura points out that it's typically the magic wand or the special powers of the female protagonist that transform her into a beauty. But the purpose of these magical transformations is not simply to become cute—it is first and foremost to defeat evil. In *Kamikaze Kaito Jeanne*, for example, sixteen-year-old schoolgirl gymnast Maron Kusakabe is reborn as Joan of Arc to battle Satan on behalf of God. Talk about high pressure!

"In the manga I used to read growing up, so many of the heroines were high school girls that I didn't even think twice about making Jeanne a high school girl," says Tanemura.

High school has traditionally been an ideal setting for many manga not simply because target readers are of high school age, but because it is an environment that provides fertile ground for stories. Not only are there many varieties of innate conflict (student versus student, student versus teacher, teenagers versus adults), there are also seemingly endless options for romance and melodrama. While varying from person to person, the school experience is one that can be considered largely universal. Readers can relate. Readers can fantasize. And not only girl readers. Shonen manga targeting male readers that are set at school or featuring schoolgirls are vast and numerous. They include Toru Fujisawa's *GTO* (*Great Teacher Onizuka*, 1997–2002), in which a twenty-two-year-old reformed hoodlum sets out to be the greatest teacher ever; Rumiko Takahashi's shonen fantasy *InuYasha: Feudal Fairytail* (1996–2008), featuring a schoolgirl transported to Japan's Warring States period (1467–1568) to battle demons; and Towa Oshima's seinen manga *High School Girls* (2001–2006), a raunchy series that is set in an all-girl high school. Takahashi and Oshima are examples of female mangaka writing in this genre—serving to proove that you don't have to be a man to be a successful writer of manga for boys.

As the new millennium dawned, female mangaka became increasingly bold with their work. Although by this time, it was getting harder to be edgy. It was no longer enough to pepper one's manga with romances between beautiful gay boys in boarding school: in order to keep up with the changing times, fantasy situations had to be replaced with situations that were seen to be tackling real issues head on. The unflinching *Confidential Confessions* (2000) from mangaka Reiko Momochi, for example, bravely took on hard-hitting themes that ranged from divorce, schoolgirl prostitution, rape, to HIV. Likewise, *Life* (2002) by Keiko Suenobu, examined up-to-the-minute issues that affect young girls, such as wrist cutting, with a storyline in which heroine Ayumu finds difficulty coping at school and begins experimenting with self-mutilation. *X-Day* (2003) by Setona Mizushiro, in a story that is somewhat less realistic, has two schoolgirls taking part in a plot to blow up their high school (although the pair later come to realize it's not their school that's the problem, but themselves).

While the vast majority of schoolgirls do not have to deal with severe issues first hand, manga such as these help to put things into perspective. Reading about a character becoming infected with HIV suddenly makes a stupid fight with friends seem insignificant. These manga allow girls to wallow in the sadness of others and hopefully feel that their own lives really aren't so rotten or their parents really that awful after all. For girls who believe that their high school experience is a nightmare, manga such as these can convince them they are not alone.

So forget the male superheroes that dominate American comic books. In Japan, it's schoolgirls. They have been with us a long time— either as heroine or supporting characters—and they will probably be around for some time to come.

"I don't think schoolgirl characters will disappear," says Osano, who has been editing manga for the past twenty years. "On the contrary, I believe they'll increase. In a peaceful era, women lead the age. And schoolgirls will continue to lead the way."

With *Sailor Moon*, *Peach Girl,* and countless other schoolgirl themed manga continuing to make their way to

What does "moé" mean?

AROUND THE YEAR 2000, as female manga readers were plunging into a gritty, often unforgiving world, male readers and anime otaku (geeks) were entering a world of warm, fuzzy cuteness. A new breed of schoolgirl characters had appeared, and they were more than simply *kawaii* (cute). They were *moé*!

The term literally means "budding," but is also a pun on "burning." Heavy on the fan service—such as putting characters in saucy outfits or providing glimpses of their underpants—moé manga and anime are not dependent on the strength of a story, but on the appeal of the characters and the mood created. The characters in *Lucky Star*, for example, break the fourth wall in a very postmodern way by making reference to the show itself—and not a whole lot else happens. While moé does not have the narrative drive of previous styles of manga and anime, it creates feelings in viewers through moments that are not clearly defined. Moé is the sum total of its parts, and in the case of anime, those moments, characters, and situations combine to create the warm fuzzy vibe that fans call "moé."

From 2005, the animation house Kyoto Animation has been specializing in moé high school characters and churning out some of the genre's biggest hits, such as in the anime adaption of the visual novel *Air*, schoolgirl rocker series *K-On!* and *The Melancholy of Haruhi Suzumiya*, starring the iconic character designed by Noizi Ito. "When I was working on the Haruhi character design, I was satisfied with the look I created," recalls Noizi, "but I had no idea just how popular that character would become in Japan and abroad." The appeal of moé, it seems, is universal.

Haruhi from
*The Melancholy
of Haruhi
Suzumiya*

*Lucky
Star*

Life by Keiko Suenobu

X-Day by Setona Mizushiro

foreign shores, international readers can't help but be exposed to these characters. This is where Western perceptions of Japanese girls are being shaped, creating images of cute, cool, and empowered girls. Schoolboys somehow lack the iconic impact and universal appeal of a young girl in a sailor suit or a school blazer.

"Schoolgirls represent possibilities," says Ueda, echoing the common theme. "They're young, they're inexperienced, they can do anything, and at that age, they have a freedom that older people don't have."

In manga and anime, Japanese schoolgirls are the embodiment of those possibilities—whether it's the possibility of falling in love, the possibility of saving the world, or the possibility of saving themselves. Their only kryptonite is growing up. ☺

Girls on the Street
on manga and anime

Shojo (girls') manga are about love, but shonen (boys') manga are all about fighting!

My favorite are *Switch Girl* and *Secret Unrequited Love* *

I like *Pokémon* and *Switch Girl*

I don't understand shonen manga. They're too hard!

Momo Abe and Rina Kitamura

ANDREW LEE

* *Secret Unrequited Love* (*Boku no Hatsukoi wo Kimi ni Sasagu*) is a love story set in high school while *Switch Girl* is about a high school girl who is a lazy, sloppy dork at home but every morning "switches on" the beautiful, popular persona her friends see at school.

© GAINAX /KHARA/ PROJECT EVA.

Rei Ayanami in her school uniform

Rei Ayanami

IN 1995, *Neon Genesis Evangelion* changed televised anime forever. The show probed the thoughts and feelings of its characters, used experimental animation techniques, and mixed various Judeo-Christian motifs—such as the cross and the tale of Adam and Eve—into a story that was complex, intriguing, and challenged viewers to think. The formula was a mainstream success, and anime in the 1990s can essentially be divided into before and after *Evangelion*.

Set in the early twenty-first century, the apocalyptic anime depicts the world in peril. A cataclysm has caused the Earth's axis to shift, causing rapid climate change, tsunamis, and ultimately killing half the Earth's population. War breaks out, and beings called Angels attack the city known as Tokyo-3. The three main characters are fourteen-year-old junior high school students—Shinji Ikari, Asuka Langley Soryu, and Rei Ayanami—who are tasked with saving the world while manning large biomechanical

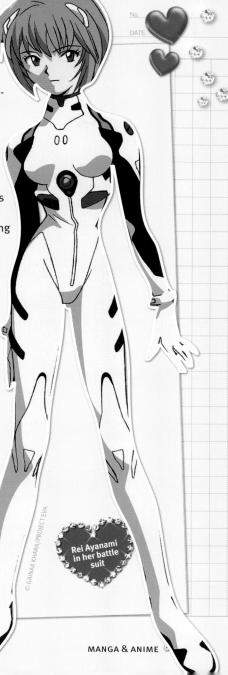

units called Evangelions. It was Shinji's fellow pilots that captured the public's imagination, and the blue-haired Rei, in particular, became the series' breakout character.

In her skin-tight battle suit or in her powder blue school uniform, the stoic, yet fragile Rei appealed to anime fans in the 1990s, and still does today. She's detached, and does not have any friends at school. Yet she's ready to follow orders and willing to risk everything to destroy the invading Angels. When the mysterious Rei first appears in the series she's injured and her head and arms are bandaged. The image of the wounded eighth grader struck a chord with viewers—she was an incredibly sympathetic character in a country that was struggling after the economic bubble burst. Rei, more than any other character, captured the melancholy mood of the nineties and epitomized Japanese ideals of loyalty, honor, and dedication.

The success of the anime led to the inevitable video game and manga spin-offs, and was a merchandising bonanza. It has even been said that the scramble for garage kit models of Rei help fuel the boom in collectable character figurines.

© GAINAX KHARA/PROJECT EVA.

Rei Ayanami
in her battle
suit

PREDATOR RAT

Ii Niku Ushijima

Cosplay queen

WITH LOOKS THAT BELIE HER AGE, Ii Niku ("Good Meat") Ushijima might be mistaken for a schoolgirl. She isn't. She is one of Japan's most famous (and controversial) cosplayers. Says Ushijima, "I cosplay schoolgirl-style characters because sailor suits and loose socks are cute."

Ii Niku Ushijima burst onto the scene in 2007. Her photos were slick, professional, and aggressively sexual. According to Ushijima, she was expressing her own fantasies. Her photos aren't just influenced by her favorite anime and manga; they are also laced with S&M references and schoolgirl iconography.

"One part of the allure of schoolgirls is that they are forbidden fruit. Another part of that allure is their own eroticism," says Ushijima. And when it come to the schoolgirl characters in anime and manga that Ushijima loves so much, it's their school uniforms that make them so darn appealing.

In February 2012, while in Taiwan for a manga and cosplay event, Ushijima's brazen style got her in hot water. "We decided to snap a photo next to a police car," she says. The photo featured her in a schoolgirl sailor suit and loose socks, flashing her panties. After she learned that her behavior had angered the Taipei cops, she quickly apologized and took down the photo. "Our goal wasn't to take a photo with the squad car—it just happened, " she says.

While her photos might look like another young woman being exploited, she produces the photos herself and self-publishes digital photo discs, which are sold in geek meccas like Tokyo's Akihabara. "I don't show anything I don't want to show," Ushijima once said, "and I don't do anything I don't want to do."

Ii Niku Ushijima as Rei Ayanami from Neon Genesis Evangelion

Go fly a kite

THE PROLIFERATION OF VCRS in the eighties and nineties saw the rise of straight-to-video anime known as OVA (original video animation). Young men, raised on giant mecha warriors in space, were keen to see *other* things, and home video was the perfect medium for anime featuring sex, extreme violence . . . and schoolgirls.

Yasuomi Umetsu made his writing and directing debut in 1998 with 18+ rated *Kite*, which was hardly a typical adult anime. After the parents of schoolgirl Sawa are brutally murdered, the young girl is taken in by corrupt cops, who turn her into an exploding bullet-packed gun wielding assassin— and their sex slave. "Actually, I wanted her to be a junior high school student," says Umetsu, "but that would have made it impossible to even get an 18+ rating." For its creator, what made the anime compelling was the contrast between the dainty schoolgirl and horrible acts of violence. "The title is a metaphor," says Umetsu. "A kite dances in the wind, controlled and manipulated by someone until the string is cut." Eventually Sawa too is able to free herself.

When it was released abroad, *Kite* was either heavily censored or banned outright, though it did develop cult status, and was shown in various international anime festivals. Quentin Tarantino drew inspiration from its heroine for the character of Gogo Yubari in his film *Kill Bill*, and pop band No Doubt paid homage to *Kite* in its music video "Ex-Girlfriend." In 2008, Umematsu followed up *Kite* with *Kite Liberator*, which tells the story of a schoolgirl named Monaka who moonlights as a pedophile-killing assassin known as the "The Angel of Death." In 2014 *Kite* was turned into a Hollywood film Starring Samuel L. Jackson and India Eisley as Sawa.

© 1998,2000 YASUOMI UMETSU/ GREEN BUNNY

Sawa, the schoolgirl assassin, in the anime *Kite*

Blood sucker

SAYA KILLS DEMONS. And does it in style in her navy blue sailor suit. She is the last vampire, star of the horror anime *Blood: The Last Vampire* from Production I.G, the studio responsible for the landmark sci-fi anime *Ghost in the Shell* and the animated sequence in *Kill Bill*.

The film is set in mid-sixties Japan, when Saya, who is hundreds of years old, is dispatched to a high school on a US forces base by a secret organization. There she uses her sword skills to slay beasts called Chiropterans in a blood soaked battle to the death.

The initial idea for *Blood* was crafted by Kenji Kamiyama and Junichi Fujisaku. Kamiyama wrote the film, while Fujisaku wrote the novelization and directed both the video game and the TV series *Blood+*. "The uniform and the *katana* (sword) communicate stoicism and evoke Japanese soldiers in wartime," says Fujisaku, who believes that the sailor suit was instrumental in creating the film's moody atmosphere.

Saya in *Blood: The Last Vampire*

Saya is, of course, just one in a long line of mighty sailor-suit–wearing heroines. Fujisaku explains the appeal: "When children are in elementary school, they see junior high and high school girls as adults, while adults view them as kids." This means for two separate audiences the "schoolgirl" has entirely different meanings—making it easier to give more complexity to a character. And all that is necessary to create a schoolgirl character is to put her in school uniform.

Graduation Day

Being a schoolgirl isn't forever. You graduate. You grow up. You trade your sailor suits for business suits or other mature trappings. The only evidence of those schoolgirl days is yearbooks, old friends, dated pics, and memories.

The schoolgal years are ephemeral. They're not tangible, unlike the impact that each successive generation has left on Japan. What doesn't change is that schoolgirls continue to dot Japan's landscape, whether that's the landscape of the country's big cities and small towns or the landscape of popular culture. They are a constant. And Japan's fascination with schoolgirls remains steadfast.

For each generation of schoolgirls the uniform symbolizes a fleeting moment in time, and trends are born as each successive group of young Japanese women strive to make their own mark, before becoming adult members of society, encumbered by new responsibilities. For many young women, these schoolgirl years are their time to let loose.

Schoolgirls represent so much in Japan. For women, schoolgirls evoke their own carefree youth. For kids, schoolgirls exist in that appealing netherworld between childhood and adulthood. For men, schoolgirls provide reminders of a time when they were still schoolboys and life was less complicated. For the country's rapidly increasing elderly, schoolgirls are not only youth, but also the future.

As the cherry blossoms fall across Japan every spring, the new school year brings a new season of schoolgirl-led fashions. Shoko and I wrote this book through admiration for these young women, who, generation after generation, rebel against conformity and assert their identity, and whose image Japan's pop culture never tires of portraying—whether through gritty realism or utter fantasy. This is the power and the cool of the Japanese schoolgirl. Long may she reign.

Brian Ashcraft

Osaka, Japan, 2014

Selected Bibliography

Anderson, Joseph L. and Donald Richie. *The Japanese Film: Art and Industry.* Princeton, NJ: Princeton University Press, 1982.

Bornoff, Nicholas. "Sex and Consumerism: The Japanese State of the Arts," in *Consuming Bodies: Sex and Contemporary Japanese Art,* ed. Fran Lloyd. London: Reaktion Books, 2002: 41–68.

——. *Pink Samurai: The Pursuit and Politics of Sex in Japan.* London: Grafton Books, 1991.

Clements, Jonathan, and Helen McCarthy. *The Anime Encyclopedia: A Guide to Japanese Animation Since 1917.* Berkeley, CA: Stone Bridge Press, 2006.

D, Chris. *Outlaw Masters of Japanese Film.* London: I.B. Tauris, 2005.

Galbraith, Patrick W. *The Otaku Encyclopedia: An Insider's Guide to the Subculture of Cool Japan.* Tokyo: Kodansha International, 2009.

Gravett, Paul. *Manga: Sixty Years of Japanese Comics.* New York: Collins Design, 2004.

Hasegawa, Yuko. "Post-identity *Kawaii*: Commerce, Gender and Contemporary Japanese Art," in *Consuming Bodies: Sex and Contemporary Japanese Art,* ed. Fran Lloyd. London: Reaktion Books, 2002: 127–141.

Inamasu, Tatsuo. *Aidoru Kougaku (Idol Engineering).* Tokyo: Chikuma Shobo, 1989.

Kinsella, Sharon. "Cuties in Japan," in *Women Media and Consumption in Japan,* eds. Lise Skov and Brian Moeran. Honolulu, HI: University of Hawai'i Press, 1995: 220–254.

——. "What's Behind the Fetishism of Japanese School Uniforms?" in *Fashion Theory,* Volume 6, Issue 2, 2002: 215–238.

Kizaki, Yoshiji and Kasumi Akaiwa. *Rock & Pops Standard 1955-64 Vol 1.* Tokyo: Ongaku Shuppansha, 2005.

Lloyd, Fran. "Strategic Interventions in Contemporary Japanese Art," in *Consuming Bodies: Sex and Contemporary Japanese Art,* ed. Fran Lloyd. London: Reaktion Books, 2002: 69–108.

Macias, Patrick, and Izumi Evers. *Japanese Schoolgirl Inferno: Tokyo Teen Fashion Subculture Handbook.* San Francisco: Chronicle Books, 2007.

Maeda, Masahiro. *Norifumi Suzuki Special HOTWAX Vol. 8.* Tokyo: Shinko Music Entertainment Co., Ltd., 2007.

Miller, Laura. "Those Naughty Teenage Girls: Japanese Kogals, Slang, and Media Assessments," in *Journal of Linguistic Anthropology*, Volume 14, Number 2, 2004: 225–242.

Miller, Laura, and Jan Bardsley, eds. *Bad Girls of Japan.* New York: Palgrave Macmillan, 2005.

Napier, Susan. "Vampires, Psychic Girls, Flying Women and Sailor Scouts: Four Faces of the Young Female in Japanese Popular Culture," in *The Worlds of Japanese Popular Culture,* ed. D.P. Martinez. Cambridge, UK: Cambridge University Press, 1998: 91–106.

Orbaugh, Sharalyn. "Busty Battlin' Babes: The Evolution of the *Shojo* in 1990s Visual Culture," in *Gender and Power: In the Japanese Visual Field,* eds. Joshua S. Mostow, Norman

Bryson, and Maribeth Graybill. Honolulu, HI: University of Hawai'i Press, 2003.

Pilling, David. "Marketing: Small, But Perfectly Funded," in *The Financial Times*. October 11, 2005.

Richie, Donald. *A Hundred Years of Japanese Film: A Concise History, with a Selective Guide to DVDs and Videos*. Tokyo: Kodansha International, 2005.

Sato, Barbara. *The New Japanese Woman: Modernity, Media, and Women in Interwar Japan*. Durham: Duke University Press, 2003.

Satsukime, Masako, ed. *Queen of Japanese Movie: From Stray Cat Rock to Girl Boss Blues. HOTWAX special edition*. Tokyo: Shinko Music Entertainment Co., Ltd., 2006.

Schilling, Mark. *No Borders, No Limits: Nikkatsu Action Cinema*. Guildford, UK: FAB Press, 2007. Honolulu, HI: University of Hawai'i Press, 2003: 201–227.

Sharp, Jasper. *Behind the Pink Curtain: The complete History of Japanese Sex Cinema*. Guildford, UK: FAB Press, 2008.

Shibuya Trend Research Group/ING, *Jidai o Tsukuru Girls' Culture: Sedai goto ni miru Jyoshi koukousei no Lifestyle*, Tokyo: Goma Books, 2006.

Sugisaku, J Taro. *Pinky Violence Tokuma Shoten*. Tokyo: Tokuma Shoten, 1999.

White, Merry. "The Marketing of Adolescence in Japan: Buying and Dreaming," in *Women Media and Consumption in Japan,* eds. Lise Skov and Brian Moeran. Honolulu, HI: University of Hawai'i Press, 1995: 255–273.

Websites

2channel
  http://www.2ch.net

Akiba Blog
  http://akibablog.net

Canned Dogs
  http://zepy.momotato.com

Danny Choo
  http://www.dannychoo.com

Encyclopedia Idollica
  http://www.idollica.com

Gigazine
  http://gigazine.net/

Kotaku
  http://kotaku.com

Japan Probe
  http://www.japanprobe.com

Matt Thorn
  http://www.matt-thorn.com

MidnightEye
  http://www.midnighteye.com

Patrick Macias
  http://patrickmacias.blogs.com

Speed Nator
  http://www.ne-ta.com

Magazines

an-an	*Otaku USA*
Bessatsu Friend	*Popteen*
Brutus	*Ribon*
Cawaii!	*Ranzuki*
CUTiE	*S Cawaii!*
Cyzo	*Shojo Friend*
Dengeki Hime	*Seventeen*
Dengeki G's Magazine	*Weekly Playboy*
egg	*Wired*
Famitsu	
*Hana*chu*	
Nakayoshi	
Newtype (Japan)	
nicola	

Index

Thanks to:

Our editor Andrew Lee without whom this project never would have happened.

Everyone at Tuttle for their support.

Everyone who was kind enough to be interviewed for this book. We truly appreciate your time, generosity, and insights.

Shinji Takenaga and the entire staff at ING for going well above and beyond the call of duty. And Saki Nishimoto for her dedicated editorial assistance.

Yohko and Yasumasa Yonehara at CexWork, Manabu Yamamoto and Junji Fukuhara at Office 48, Hirofumi Abe and Takahiro Ando at Space Craft Group, Kenji Kawakami at Tombow. Kenichi Minoda at Softpal, Fumio Osano and Toshiyuki Tanaka at Kodansha, Eiki Yoshimine at Sony Music, Eisuke Taga at Kitty, Takako Yamamoto and Eri Inagaki at Epic Records Japan, Motohisa Nagata at Office Walker, Ami Fukuda at MEM Gallery, Eriko Kusaka at Mizuma Art Gallery, Maya Shishikura at Prap Japan, Rie Waki at eg5 management, Naoi Takatoshi at Spotted Productions, Up Front Agency, Masanori Koike at Arms, Motohiro Ichikawa at Top Coat, and Toyoko Yokoyama at Conomi.

Patrick W. Galbraith, Philomena Keet, Franceso Fondi, Mari Oda, Hinako Sugioka, Mie Miyashita, Naoko Takeuchi, Production I.G, Capcom USA, Hakugen, Fukuoka Jo Gakuin, Conomi, SNK Playmore, Bandai, the Ministry of Foreign Affairs, KariAng, Popteen, Shueisha, rienda, the Writers Guild of Japan, GAGA Communications, D3P, Nikkatsu, Toei, Toho, Hori Pro, nicola, Knax, HuneX, Shibuya 109, Fuyru, Japan Rail, Sony Music Direct, Moon the Child, Avex, K press, Geneon Universal Entertainment Japan, Aquaplus, Ganiax, Sanrio, Niigata College of Art & Design, Aniplex, Pony Canyon, Kaikai Kiki, WIX, E.G Smith, Kadokawa Pictures, and NTT DoCoMo.

Brian Crecente, Michael Fahey, Michael McWhertor, Luke Plunkett, Stephen Totilo, Owen Good, and Kotaku. Nick Denton and everyone at Gawker Media. Chris Baker and *Wired* magazine. Sonia Zjawinski, Patrick Macias, Jean Snow, Jason Chen, Dixie Xue, Jeff Pash, Suzy Cho, Matt Alt, David Abrams, Brendan I. Koerner, Denki, Rolling Thunder Pictures, Jerry Martinez, Andrew Crooke, Daniel Barber, and Stephen Park.

Our parents, Idzuhiko and Kyoko Ueda, Ronald and Joy Ashcraft. And of course, Taro, Kouta, and Serina as well as the entire Bamboo Family.

Our children, Ren, Louis, and the new baby, for putting up with two busy parents during the course of this book.

And lastly, the schoolgirls of Japan for being so damn cool.

Brian Ashcraft and **Shoko Ueda**
Osaka, 2014

The Tuttle Story: "Books to Span the East and West"

Many people are surprised to learn that the world's largest publisher of books on Asia had its humble beginnings in the tiny American state of Vermont. The company's founder, Charles Tuttle, came from a New England family steeped in publishing.

Tuttle's father was a noted antiquarian dealer in Rutland, Vermont. Young Charles honed his knowledge of the trade working in the family bookstore, and later in the rare books section of Columbia University Library. His passion for beautiful books—old and new—never wavered throughout his long career as a bookseller and publisher.

After graduating from Harvard, Tuttle enlisted in the military and in 1945 was sent to Tokyo to work on General Douglas MacArthur's staff. He was tasked with helping to revive the Japanese publishing industry, which had been utterly devastated by the war. When his tour of duty was completed, he left the military, married a talented and beautiful singer, Reiko Chiba, and in 1948 began several successful business ventures.

To his astonishment, Tuttle discovered that postwar Tokyo was actually a book-lover's paradise. He befriended dealers in the Kanda district and began supplying rare Japanese editions to American libraries. He also imported American books to sell to the thousands of GIs stationed in Japan. By 1949, Tuttle's business was thriving, and he opened Tokyo's very first English-language bookstore in the Takashimaya Department Store in Ginza, to great success. Two years later, he began publishing books to fulfill the growing interest of foreigners in all things Asian.

Though a westerner, Tuttle was hugely instrumental in bringing a knowledge of Japan and Asia to a world hungry for information about the East. By the time of his death in 1993, he had published over 6,000 books on Asian culture, history and art—a legacy honored by Emperor Hirohito in 1983 with the "Order of the Sacred Treasure," the highest honor Japan can bestow upon non-Japanese.

The Tuttle company today maintains an active backlist of some 1,500 titles, many of which have been continuously in print since the 1950s and 1960s—a great testament to Charles Tuttle's skill as a publisher. More than 60 years after its founding, Tuttle Publishing is more active today than at any time in its history, still inspired by Charles Tuttle's core mission—to publish fine books to span the East and West and provide a greater understanding of each.